PSYCHOLOGY

PSYCHOLOGY 101½

THE UNSPOKEN RULES FOR SUCCESS IN ACADEMIA

SECOND EDITION

ROBERT J. STERNBERG

AMERICAN PSYCHOLOGICAL ASSOCIATION
WASHINGTON, DC

Published by
American Psychological Association
750 First Street, NE
Washington, DC 20002
www.apa.org

To order
APA Order Department
P.O. Box 92984
Washington, DC 20090-2984
Tel: (800) 374-2721; Direct: (202) 336-5510
Fax: (202) 336-5502; TDD/TTY: (202) 336-6123
Online: www.apa.org/pubs/books
E-mail: order@apa.org

In the U.K., Europe, Africa, and the Middle East, copies may be ordered from
American Psychological Association
3 Henrietta Street
Covent Garden, London
WC2E 8LU England

Typeset in Sabon by Circle Graphics, Inc., Columbia, MD

Printer: Maple Press, York, PA
Cover Designer: Beth Schlenoff Design, Bethesda, MD

The opinions and statements published are the responsibility of the authors, and such opinions and statements do not necessarily represent the policies of the American Psychological Association.

Library of Congress Cataloging-in-Publication Data

Names: Sternberg, Robert J., author.
Title: Psychology 101 1/2 : the unspoken rules for success in academia / Robert J. Sternberg.
Description: Second edition. | Washington, DC : American Psychological Association, [2017] | Includes bibliographical references and index.
Identifiers: LCCN 2016000181 | ISBN 9781433822490 | ISBN 1433822490
Subjects: LCSH: Psychology—Study and teaching (Higher) | Psychology—Study and teaching (Graduate)
Classification: LCC BF77 .S68 2017 | DDC 150.71/1—dc23 LC record available at http://lccn.loc.gov/2016000181

British Library Cataloguing-in-Publication Data
A CIP record is available from the British Library.

Printed in the United States of America
Second Edition

http://dx.doi.org/10.1037/14949-000

This book is dedicated to my primary mentors in my career—
Endel Tulving, Gordon Bower, and the late Wendell Garner.
I thank them sincerely and with all my heart for all the
valuable lessons about career and life
I have learned from them.

Contents

Preface

More than a decade ago, I had an idea for a book that I eventually wrote and titled *Psychology 101½: The Unspoken Rules for Success in Academia*. In a nutshell, my concern was that young career scientists in psychology often did not learn in graduate school or through postdoctoral experience the important knowledge they would need to make a success of their careers; I certainly didn't. They usually did learn the formal, explicit knowledge of the field. What was missing was the informal, implicit, and often unspoken (or tacit) knowledge upon which careers are built—how one can organize oneself and one's resources to succeed in a challenging and competitive field.

I have written this book primarily for graduate students, postdocs, and early-career scientists, but I suspect that even some later career scientists may find something to learn. I believe the book may be of use for first-year proseminars and also for courses on professional issues that are taught in some psychology departments and in other departments that embrace psychological science. Each lesson is presented in a way so as to make four basic points, although the format is varied to preserve the interest of the text: (a) the lesson, (b) how and where I learned it, (c) why it is important, and (d) one or more concrete examples of it. All of the concrete examples are real and from my career or those of other people I have known personally.

So why a second edition of a book that has done well?

First, I am now older and, I believe, perhaps a wee bit wiser. When I wrote the first edition, my entire career had been spent at Yale (with the exception of 3 years of graduate school at Stanford). I now have had the privilege of serving for some time as well at Tufts University, Oklahoma State University, and Cornell University, and my knowledge of university settings is broader than it was then and, perhaps, even a bit deeper. I also have since been president of the American Psychological Association (APA), the Eastern Psychological Association, and the Federation of Associations in Behavioral and Brain Sciences, and as a result, I have learned a great deal about the field of psychology that I just didn't know back at the turn of the 21st century.

Second, the field of psychology has changed enormously in the 12 years since APA published the first edition. Many journals have gone either fully or partially electronic; grants have become scarcer; funding has become more directed toward specific topics; teaching has become more multimodal; scientists have come to be rated on new quantitative scales (e.g., *H*—the number of publications *H* one has that have been cited *H* times); journals have come to be rated for "impact"; and new forms of promoting ideas, such as blogs, have become available. Moreover, as the number of aspiring academics has increased, the field has become just a lot more competitive. I came to believe that the first edition of the book no longer fully reflected current realities.

Third, the lessons in the first edition were presented in a more or less random order, making it harder for readers fully to profit from the book. In this edition, I have ordered the lessons into five parts: Identity and Integrity (Part I), Interpersonal Relationships (Part II), Institutions and Academia (Part III), Problems and Tasks (Part IV), and Job and Career (Part V).

Fourth, and perhaps most important, I realized that something fundamental was missing in the first edition: pedagogy. I thought the greatest challenge was simply in knowing the unspoken rules for success in academia. But I came to realize, over the course of time, that even harder than knowing the rules is reflecting on these rules and knowing how to apply them. One may think one is doing what needs to be done at the same time that no one else thinks so. As a result, in this edition, I present for each lesson (except 101½) two kinds of supportive pedagogy in the form of questions:

- *Think For Yourself:* These questions ask the reader to think about the issue discussed in the lesson and to reflect in the abstract on an aspect of it. They ensure that the reader has understood the basic content of the lesson.

- *Put It Into Practice:* These questions ask the reader to apply an aspect of the lesson to his or her own career. They ensure that the reader sees how the particular lesson applies to his or her personal experiences of career development.

In using this book, keep three things in mind. First, there is no recipe for success that works for everyone. Learning the lessons in this book will help you get where you want to go, but it will not get you there. You have to get yourself there. Second, do not let yourself become discouraged by the large number of ways in which you need improvement. I have been in the field for 40 years, and I still have innumerable ways in which I can improve. Self-improvement is a lifelong course, not a quick fix. Finally, look at the 101½ lessons in this book not as obstacles but as opportunities: They provide you with shortcuts to attaining your goals, whatever those goals may be.

I hope that, whoever you are, your career and your life will be changed for the better by reading this book. Let me know. I'd be delighted to hear from you via e-mail (robert.sternberg@cornell.edu).

I
Identity and Integrity

Lesson 1
Don't Believe Things Just Because Other People Do

Endel Tulving has made a career of defying people's expectations. When most people believed that merely repeating a word would increase recall for that word because increased frequency should result in increased retrieval of the word, Tulving (1966) showed that under certain circumstances, increased repetitions of a word could actually impair recall of the word. When most people believed that recognition memory must be better than recall memory, Tulving performed a series of experiments showing that recall memory could be better than recognition memory (Tulving & Thomson, 1973).

A major lesson I learned from Tulving was that just because many people believe something does not make it true. On the contrary, Tulving has tended throughout his career to be skeptical of things that a lot of people believe.

It is not only Tulving who has capitalized on defying people's expectations. Martin Seligman (in press) has written of how, when he first proposed positive psychology, with its focus on positive events in people's lives and on people's future lives rather than their past lives, he was met with stony silence by psychologists whom he addressed at a meeting of a group of members of the American Psychological Association. Today, positive psychology is one of the larger subfields of psychology and is widely accepted and applauded.

When I was young—back in the 1950s—there was a time when every kid had a hula hoop. If you did not have one, you were, well, nobody. A few years later, everyone had put away his or her hula hoop. The new fad was yo-yos. Everyone just had to have a yo-yo. If you didn't, horrible things would happen to you, at least in your social circles. Hula hoops never came back—not yet, anyway. Yo-yos did—briefly—and then scooters were the rage. Then that fad passed, to be replaced by another, and then another.

Many of us who entered scientific careers did so because we thought we were putting the fad-purchasing mentality behind us. We may have been nonconformists as children—and perhaps as adults as well—and therefore have found the practice of keeping up with the Joneses somewhat repugnant.

Yet, some cancellation principle may be at work, whereby when one puts a bunch of nonconformists together into a field, their nonconformities somehow cancel each other out. As Thomas Kuhn (2012) argued, science seems to survive, to a large extent, on the kind of conformity many of its practitioners thought they had rejected.

Of course, the fact that a lot of people believe something does not make it wrong. The important point is that you seek answers for yourself. Don't be content to believe something just because other people do. Think for yourself, and you will be on the road to success in science.

This lesson is not an exercise in playing holier than thou. As you will see throughout this book, I have learned many of these lessons the hard way—through my mistakes! And although I never felt the need to study a hot topic just because it was hot, I certainly have followed fads. I had a hula hoop when I was in first grade. Then I had a yo-yo when I was in sixth grade. But I never had a scooter. I hope I have outgrown my need to follow fads. Shouldn't we all?

THINK FOR YOURSELF: *Why do scientists sometimes follow fads? What is adaptive about their doing so? What is maladaptive?*

PUT IT INTO PRACTICE: *Do I know why I'm doing what I'm doing? Am I doing what I am doing because it is what I want to do or because others are pressuring me to do it? Do I believe in what I'm doing?*

Lesson 2

When You Make Mistakes, Admit Them, Learn From Them, and Move On

Everyone makes mistakes. I do; you do; all the people you know about and care about do. Making mistakes is not in itself a source of variation among individuals, although certainly some people may make more than others. What is a source of variation is the extent to which people are willing to admit to their mistakes, learn from them, and move on. In our work on practical intelligence (e.g., Cianciolo, Matthew, Sternberg, & Wagner, 2006; Sternberg et al., 2000), we have found that the people who are the most successful often are those who admit to, and learn from, mistakes. They are not necessarily the people with the highest IQs. In general, I have found that people who are unable or unwilling to admit mistakes, and who react defensively to criticism, no matter how constructive it is, have a relatively poor prognosis for success in the field.

The problem with not admitting mistakes is that the mistakes you make to which you do not admit are likely to keep coming back to you. They never pass you by because you have not allowed yourself to put them behind you and move on.

In my lab over the years, people who have been unable to admit to mistakes have never worked out well. They have trouble getting their articles accepted because they ignore feedback from referees. They have trouble getting funded because, when they revise their grant proposals, the proposals look to reviewers pretty much like the earlier versions did. And they have trouble working with other people because they keep making the same mistakes in their interactions with others.

One of the more serious cases I have seen of someone who could not admit to mistakes was that of a member of a psychology faculty who was exploitative of other people—students, schools in which she worked, even other faculty. The exploitation was rather blatant. Relationships for her were clearly defined by what was in them for her. She was unwise, in the sense that she pretty much considered only her own interests and not the interests of others or of the institution. Students complained, and even school districts complained, and she received detailed and repeated feedback. But her reaction was to blame the messenger bringing the bad news and to insist that there was an organized conspiracy against her. It never was clear who was behind the conspiracy or why they would have fomented it. But she never changed her views, was encouraged to leave, and eventually left. Exploiting others is always a mistake, and she seemed to be either unable to recognize this fact or unable to recognize her own tendency to engage in it. She made a mistake, and then made it again and again and again. Don't you do the same!

It is important in your career to not only admit to your mistakes but to also take responsibility for them and for their consequences. People who take responsibility for their actions are more likely to learn from them and thus to improve the way they function. People who seek to blame others, or who simply are not willing to take responsibility for what they have done, do not quite recognize that they have a problem and hence are unable fully to address and ultimately to resolve it.

Like most people, I suppose, I've made some fairly serious mistakes in my life. One that comes to mind is hiring someone who had appeared right for the job but rather rapidly proved to be a mistake. I should have let him go quickly. I didn't and came later deeply to regret it because he made life hard not only for me but also for everyone else in my group. Had I admitted the mistake more quickly, a lot of people would have been much happier with their work environment.

◻ ◻ ◻ ◻ ◻ ◻ ◻

THINK FOR YOURSELF: *Why, when people make mistakes, are they so unwilling to admit to them, not only to themselves but also to other people?*

PUT IT INTO PRACTICE: *Have you in the past made mistakes that you were reluctant to admit? How about now? Are you making mistakes that you refuse to face up to? What are you going to do about it?*

Lesson 3

Decide What Is Important to You, and Then Be True to It

I learned this lesson from Wendell Garner, my informal senior-faculty mentor when I was a junior faculty member at Yale. It's important to follow this lesson because if you let the important things go—the things you really stand for—soon you may find yourself standing for nothing. The things that are really important to you largely define who you are, and in letting go of them, in an important sense, you give up on yourself.

During my fifth year as an assistant professor, I was being considered for an appointment as a tenured associate professor in the Department of Psychology at Yale. Yale, like many other universities, seeks opinions from external referees to guide it in the rendering of tenure decisions. Thus, it was important to impress senior people not only within the university but also outside of it.

I began to hear rumors that some of the external letters that were coming in were skeptical about my defining myself as being in the field of human intelligence. Fields within psychology, as within any science, have different levels of prestige, and intelligence has tended over the years to be toward the bottom of the ladder of prestige. One can see this by the fact that few graduate programs focus on human intelligence, and almost no jobs are defined as being in the field of human intelligence.

When I heard about the referees' letters, I felt close to a state of panic. How could I have made such a dumb decision regarding the field in which

I worked? I sought out Garner and told him that I thought I had made a dreadful mistake. I had realized that I could have done exactly the same work I had been doing all along, but I could have called it something else or I could have worked in another field. Perhaps I should have worked in a field that I cared less about so that referees would have been more positive. Maybe I still could change fields.

Garner heard me out, and then gave me some of the best advice I ever have gotten. He said, in essence, that I had entered psychology and then come to Yale with the mission of wanting to make a difference to the field of intelligence. Now I was afraid that this mission would cost me my job. I was right, he said, in thinking that it might cost me my job. But the right thing for me to do was to continue to define myself as being in the field of intelligence. The reason was that my mission was extremely important to me—it was what I cared about—and so I had to follow it, even if it cost me my job. If I wanted to go into some other field, it should be because I want to study that field, not just to gain the referees' approval.

I realized he was right, and I continued to define myself as being in the field of intelligence. And I got tenure. I might not have. But I realized that there was no room for compromise on something so important to me, and that this was the only position I could take.

There are times in a career when one has to call one's work by different names to achieve the outcomes one desires. For example, if a request for grant proposals is in the field of problem solving, and I study intelligence, I will have no trouble calling my work in the field of intelligence "problem solving," because problem solving is an integral and necessary part of intelligence. So are "reasoning," "concept formation," and many other related constructs. So long as I know what I believe in and what I care about, the terminology is secondary to what the research is actually about. Investigators of intelligence necessarily study these other phenomena. Similarly, if one is interested in close relationships, one could easily call one's work many other things—intimate relationships, personal relationships, and so forth—without compromising the integrity of what one is doing. The main thing is to ensure one is being true to oneself—and, of course, to the mission of the granting agency that issued the request for grant proposals.

In another experience, I was leading a large academic unit that was not known for its academic excellence. I told people in the unit that not only could the unit be good but it could actually be great at what it did. I thought people would be thrilled to hear the message. They weren't; they accused me of lying. The thought of transformational change—of becoming really great—was not in their plans. The members of the unit were very happy to stay just the way they were. I decided to get out of the post: It didn't fit who I was or what I hoped to do.

During the course of a career, there are always temptations to abandon things you deeply believe in. You may deeply believe in teaching but find that most of the rewards are for research, or vice versa. You may deeply believe in a certain approach to a problem that just happens not to be popular in your department. The temptations to sell out are enormous, and the rewards seemingly large. But selling out may or may not get one the rewards one seeks; it always loses one the most important reward of all: a sense of personal identity and integrity.

Find people you admire and emulate them. You don't need to emulate them for their particular research topics or styles, but do it for their integrity. And if you can't find such people, at the very least decide to become one yourself so that others in turn can emulate you down the road.

THINK FOR YOURSELF: *Should granting agencies define acceptable topics for grants narrowly, thereby acquiring proposals they may want but possibly at the expense of researchers doing research in which they are less interested?*

PUT IT INTO PRACTICE: *Do you actually know what is important to you? Do you know how to accomplish these things? Are you sure that the things that you have named as important to you are truly important to you, or are they things that others want for you?*

Lesson 4
Delay Gratification

Part of being successful means being able to work on a project or task for a long time without immediate or interim rewards. Rewards are not always immediate, and delaying gratification usually has benefits. The fact of the matter is that in the short term, people are often ignored when they do creative work or are even punished for doing it.

Many people believe that they should be rewarded immediately for good performance, and that it is always reasonable to expect quick rewards. Not so.

In psychology, you often have to wait for rewards. The greatest rewards are often those that are delayed (Mischel, 2014). I can relate to the concept of delayed gratification, as one of the greatest rewards of my own life has yet to come. Some years ago I contracted with a publisher to develop a test of intelligence based on my theory of intelligence (Sternberg, 1985). Things were going well until the president of the company left and a new president took over. Shortly after that, my project was canceled. The company's perception was that there was not enough of a potential market for a test of intelligence founded on my theory of analytical, creative, and practical abilities. My perception was that the company and some of its market were stuck in the past, endlessly replicating the construction and use of the kinds of tests that had been constructed and used since the turn of the 20th century. From my point of view, it is hard to find an industry less creative than the testing industry, at least given the rate of innovation they have shown to date.

Some years later, we are still working to find a way that others can use the test. It is a difficult exercise in delay of gratification. But I try to practice what I preach, and so I wait for the day when the test will see the light of day and make a difference to children's lives.

We all have different tolerances for delaying gratification. Where this issue becomes crucial is in submitting articles to journals. When I submitted an article based on my dissertation, I faced a typical problem: Do I submit the article to a top journal and risk multiple rounds of review, with an uncomfortably high probability of the article's ultimately being rejected? Or do I submit it to a less prestigious journal, where hopefully its chances of an acceptance and even a relatively quick acceptance are much higher? I went for the better journal and am glad I did. In fact, the article did go through multiple rounds of review, and it was not clear until the end that it would be accepted. But the final result was worth waiting for.

Delay of gratification always has to be balanced with the need for shorter term rewards. For example, a faculty member coming up for tenure typically can afford to delay gratification only so long in getting articles accepted by journals. With journal submissions, therefore, one may sometimes have to settle for a less prestigious journal or other outlet because of time pressure.

◫ ◫ ◫ ◫ ◫ ◫ ◫

THINK FOR YOURSELF: *Why do people so often go for short-term rewards rather than waiting for the longer term ones?*

PUT IT INTO PRACTICE: *Are you willing to wait longer for better outcomes? If not, why not? What kinds of steps could you take to increase your willingness to delay gratification and thus achieve better outcomes in your life?*

Lesson 5
Do What You Believe Is Right

In 2001, I decided to run for president of the American Psychological Association (APA) and try to win for the 2003 election. I had been president of four APA divisions, and I thought that I was up to the challenge. Because five candidates run in each election and because all are typically very prominent psychologists, it is difficult to win this election. If one wishes to win, then one has to set one's mind to it and make a serious effort.

Fairly early during the campaign period, a very difficult situation arose in the APA (see Sternberg, 2002a) with regard to an article submitted for publication. A well-known psychologist wrote an article that was somewhat critical of the APA. The author of the article received from the APA editor what he reasonably believed to be an acceptance of his article, and even a letter congratulating him on the article's acceptance. Then the apparent acceptance was rendered conditional by a higher level APA editor who asked the author to make substantial revisions. The author sent an e-mail to several individuals expressing his view of events and his outrage.

The e-mail was widely circulated, and soon a storm was brewing. Prominent scientists came to the defense of the author and expressed their dissatisfaction with the way the APA had handled the publishing situation. Some of the postings in the e-mail threads were downright hostile toward APA and the various APA officials involved. The volume and intensity of the e-mail correspondence increased, and members of one prominent psychology department—Harvard—even signed a joint protest letter.

At that point, I found myself in a dilemma. I sympathized with the author: Clearly, the handling of his manuscript left much to be desired. Something had gone wrong. But, at the same time, the author had instituted an appeal process, and it seemed to me that he might have waited until the result of the appeal was determined before he sent his aforementioned outraged e-mail to several individuals. Moreover, it seemed that even if his point of view were totally justified, psychologists owed it to themselves to hear the point of view of the editor who qualified the original editorial decision. The editor had not yet responded to the author's appeal, in part because of the confidentiality that needs to be honored toward authors and reviewers.

The question was whether I should get myself involved in what had become a very hot argument. Pretty much everyone I spoke to said that I should stay out of it. After all, it was a no-win situation. No matter what I said, I would antagonize a large group of people, and worse, they were people who, under other circumstances, might vote for me. The best thing, it seemed, was just to stay out of it (as the other candidates appeared to be doing).

I gave it a great deal of thought and finally decided I had to speak up, even if it cost me the election. If I did not speak up when I had something to say, then I would feel that, even if I won the election, it would be a hollow victory: I would have won by selling myself out. I decided I would rather say what I believed and lose the election than stay silent at a time of crisis. So I made a series of postings on a widely read LISTSERV.

The results were mixed. Several individuals wrote back to express their agreement with what I had said and their thanks for my having said it. Other individuals wrote back to disagree, in some cases, vociferously. And a few people wrote back to say, in essence, that they would rather vote for the devil than for me. I believe I made more friends than enemies, but who knows? Ultimately, I won the APA election, and was glad I spoke out, because I had done what I believed one must do for important issues: Do what one believes is right, and let the chips fall where they may.

Sometimes the chips do not fall exactly as one might wish. I once had an employee who was, in my opinion, ineffective in his work and destructive for the morale of the group. When the grant on which he was working came to an end, I terminated his employment because I had no work I believed he would perform satisfactorily. I knew that the termination would not make him happy. Indeed, the less competent employees are sometimes those who cling most steadfastly to their jobs because it often is not so easy for them to be hired elsewhere. When I let him go, he decided to file a grievance with the union. At that point, I had to decide whether to subject myself to a grievance hearing—which I definitely did not relish—or somehow try to find work for the employee. I decided to go ahead with the hearing. I simply had nothing that I thought he could do satisfactorily, and so I believed it appropriate that when the grant on which he was working came to an end, so did his employment. I went to the grievance hearing, and won my case. Had I chickened out, I would have been left with an employee whose work was not satisfactory and whose effect on morale was, in my view, deleterious.

▣ ▣ ▣ ▣ ▣ ▣ ▣

THINK FOR YOURSELF: *What are some of the reasons that when people know what the right thing to do is, they don't do it?*

PUT IT INTO PRACTICE: *Do you stick up for what you believe in? If not, why not? Would you have more pride in yourself if you did stick up for your beliefs? How could you change your behavior so that you would be true to yourself in the future?*

Lesson 6

Be Not a Saint, a Sinner, or a Sucker

We sometimes hear that the best path through life is a "middle way"—some hypothetical mean that guides you away from extremes. I believe that much can be said for finding such a middle way. Certainly this is true with regard to three traps psychologists sometimes fall into.

The first is the nobly motivated desire to be a "saint." In the course of your career, you receive interminable demands from many people for your time. In a typical day, for example, I get perhaps 100 to 150 e-mails. Some, but not many, of them are essential. Among the nonessential are some that are worth my time and many others that are not. I often find the types of e-mail requests listed below.

- Requests from high school, college, and sometimes graduate students for help on class papers, which usually are conveniently due the next day so they kindly request an immediate response. A typical e-mail of this kind lists five to 10 questions, all of which could be answered by reading even one of the many things I've written. But why bother to read anything when you can get a personal response from the author of the papers and save yourself the time of actually doing library research? I usually do write back to such individuals, but only to suggest they read one or two works that I will specify. I've always felt it was highly unlikely that they will read anything. More likely, they will try to find some other person who is willing to respond at length to their e-mail. In my view, such a response would place me in the "sucker," not the saint, category. It is not my responsibility—or yours—to write student papers for the students who are supposed to be writing them. So I avoid the temptation to play saint, because I would not really be a saint if I helped them.

- Requests from parents and other guardians for help with a personal problem they or their children are having. Often, I will get fairly lengthy descriptions of such problems from people I do not know. I sometimes will say something vague but then will suggest that the individual get professional help. Although you may feel like you are being a saint to respond at length to such queries, you actually are being either a sucker or, as likely, a "sinner." First, if you are not licensed, you have no business giving anyone advice in your role as a psychologist. The only license I have is a driver's license, and that license, for better or worse, does not authorize me to give advice. Giving advice in your role as a psychologist if you are unlicensed is an ethically and legally questionable move. Second, no matter how much detail you receive in these e-mails (or letters or phone calls), it will almost never be enough for you to provide the kind of advice the person needs. The individual typically needs professional counseling, not a stab in the dark as to how you can help him or her. So you may think you are being helpful, but you perhaps really are not being helpful at all, and you may even be hurtful. Third, you may find yourself getting into what you thought was a one-round interchange but what the correspondent sees as a continuing exchange of letters. More than once, I have been in a situation in which I answered one e-mail (even briefly), only to find that, for the correspondent, this was the beginning of a long round of letters, not just a single one. You therefore need to take care that you do not get sucked into an endless interchange. Again, what seems like sainthood is not.
- Spam. Just delete it. Don't even consider replying, even to complain or to criticize the sender. Once you reply, you have identified your-self as an interested party, and you never know how many people your e-mail address will be sold to. Responding in any way is likely simply to generate more e-mail, not less.

There are other ways in which you can find yourself becoming a sucker when you thought you were being a saint. Sometimes you will get requests for assistance from colleagues whom you do know. I typically respond favorably to such requests. I want to help out any colleague I can. But in the course of a career, one inevitably runs into people who do not know when to stop: Having received a favorable response to one request for help, they keep coming back, again and again, and soon you become sucked into being a source of help to someone who has managed to attach himself or herself to you in a parasitic way. Often, one cannot tell in advance who these people are. And often, as well, the requests are so plaintive and the person so seemingly in need of further and further help that it is hard to say no. In these cases, painful though it can be, I believe you need to back off. I find relatively few such people but enough to realize that if I am not on my guard, I can begin to attract more and more of them and to have less and less time both for my own work and for helping people who genuinely do need help.

Some people in academia truly seem like saints. They are always helping others at the expense of their own career. This is as bad a way to go as never helping other people. Many such people have difficulty getting promoted. Even if they do get promoted, they then have difficulty establishing a reputation for themselves. In the long run, they are less able to help others because they have not established their own careers. You need to look out for yourself, and for others, but neither to the exclusion of the other.

One way to look out for yourself is to realize that things are not always as they appear to be on the surface. One of the ways people can sucker themselves out is to believe that the deep structure of a place is the same as its surface structure. Consider a simple example. When I was hired as an assistant professor, on the surface, I was hired to teach. My contractual obligation concerned appearing for a certain number of classes and teaching them successfully. But the main way I was evaluated was not on the basis of what I nominally was hired to do. The main way I was evaluated was for my research. The same would be true at most research-oriented universities: Teaching counts, but research counts more. So the surface structure of the culture concerns teaching, but the deep structure concerns and values research at least as much as, and probably more than, teaching. As Chris Argyris (2012) would have said, sometimes the espoused theory is not the theory in use: What people say may not be what they do.

Consider a second example, which applies to individuals rather than organizations. I work in the field of intelligence, broadly defined. An important part of this field is the study of critical and creative thinking. Several investigators in my field specialize in one or both of these types of thinking. They will go from one venue to another, exhorting their audiences on the value of critical thinking. One of them, in particular, has many devotees of his way of teaching critical thinking. Some view him as something of a guru in this field. But here is the rub. When you use his methods, he insists that you use them in exactly the way he prescribes. If you diverge from the approved way of using his materials, then you are, in effect, kicked out of his inner circle. The irony of what he is doing seems to escape him. He encourages people, in the abstract, to think critically. But that encouragement seems not to apply to his devotees. Them he expects to follow him slavishly, or be excommunicated from his group. The theory he espouses is greatly at variance with the theory he uses.

In sum, it is important to be on the lookout both for what people say and what they do. Do not assume that the two are the same, because often they do not correspond. If you want to know what is valued—what the tacit knowledge of an environment is—look for what really is rewarded, not just for what people say is rewarded. And then decide whether the reward system is for you. If it is not, make every effort to find another environment in which to function. You will be happier if you do.

▣ ▣ ▣ ▣ ▣ ▣ ▣

THINK FOR YOURSELF: *What are the risks of professional selfishness? How can it be risky also to be too selfless?*

PUT IT INTO PRACTICE: *Do people sometimes take advantage of you? Do you let them? How can you change that behavior? Do you sometimes take advantage of others? How can you change that?*

Lesson 7
Believe in Yourself and Yours

In any career there come times when you feel that many people, perhaps most people, do not believe in you. It may be that you are going through a period of having conflict with others; that you have an idea that you really like but no one else seems to; that you get a string of articles or grant proposals turned down, or perhaps both; or that you simply are chronically insecure. But such times should be expected in every career.

I've had many such periods. At one point, I came out of a string of grant proposals that had been turned down. I found myself wondering whether perhaps my research program was washed up, or at least perceived that way. Then, finally, I got a proposal funded and at a high level. Other times, I've had one article after another rejected. When I was being considered for tenure, I went through a very hard time (as do many people), and then someone very close to me at the time but outside the field of psychology commented that maybe I wasn't so hot after all—after all, this person commented, he had only my word that my work was any good. Years later, this same individual commented that he had heard from someone in the field that I had retreated into obscurity, and I found myself agreeing. Bad idea! I never should have agreed with him. No matter how bad things get, it is extremely important never to lose confidence in yourself—to come to believe that you really can't do much of anything.

Psychology 101½: The Unspoken Rules for Success in Academia, Second Edition, by R. J. Sternberg
Copyright © 2017 by the American Psychological Association. All rights reserved.

Strictly speaking, I refer here to loss of what sometimes is called self-efficacy, not self-esteem. *Self-efficacy* refers to your belief that you can accomplish the tasks you need to accomplish, whereas *self-esteem* refers to a more generalized high opinion of oneself that is not necessarily linked to task performance. Once you lose your or self-efficacy, you have nothing to keep you going.

For some reason, much—and I suspect, most—of the feedback people get in the field of psychology is negative. Acceptance rates of articles by journals are very low, which means that most people are going to get their articles turned down most of the time. Grant funding is very limited, and in the typical grants competition, many more people are turned down than are funded. Additionally, students are often very demanding, and those who are most likely to come to you with comments are the dissatisfied students.

Dean Simonton (1997, 2004) has found that, as creative individuals grow older, they become less and less productive. There may be several reasons for decreasing productivity. They may be busy in managerial or committee roles; they may be spending more time on teaching; they may be intellectually or even physically exhausted. But one thing I see commonly is that they become scared. They learn that eminence is no protector against critical feedback, and they may stop producing because they have tenure and do not need to produce, and because often it is even more embarrassing to receive negative reviews of your work later in your career than it is to receive them earlier. So they may become self-protective, and give up. Why expose themselves to ridicule? You don't have to be old to lose your creativity. All you have to do is become scared of trying out new things. People can become scared at 60, or they can become scared at 30 or even 25. It's up to you to retain your openness to new challenges, regardless of your age.

Simonton is a premier researcher in the field of creativity. He perhaps studies creativity in part because of his own experiences. He described to me (personal communication, February 9, 2000) how, when he was in graduate school, he was roundly criticized by some of his professors for the kind of historiometric work (i.e., quantitative studies based on historical documents and records) he was starting to do in his studies of creativity. One professor told Simonton that he never would achieve

22

even one publication in a first-rate journal. Had Simonton lost faith in himself, he never would have continued with the research that has landed him numerous publications in first-rate journals and made him one of the most widely cited psychologists in the field of creativity, or in any field.

Often, once you start losing confidence in yourself, it is difficult to turn back because you create a self-fulfilling prophecy. If you do not believe in yourself, you often convey that attitude to others, who may stop believing in you as well. You often act in ways that do not inspire confidence in others. So you become a loser not because you originally were, but because you thought you were.

Some years ago, I was invited to give a talk in a rather rough section of a large city. I was quite worried about the whole prospect, especially because the talk was to be given at night and by the time I was done and left, it would be dark. I was driving, and worried about getting lost. I felt I had a lousy sense of direction, and if anyone would get lost, it would be me. This all happened, of course, in pre-GPS days.

I drove to the school where I was to give the talk, carefully following the complex directions I had been given and paying attention to all the numerous twists and turns in the roads. I got to the school without much trouble. At the end of the talk, I had to return along the reverse of the route I had taken to get to the school. I could no longer read the directions because it was too dark. What would happen if I got lost?

I left the talk, carefully paid attention to the streets, and got out of the rough section of town without a hitch. I then realized something about myself. I had always told myself I lack a sense of direction. As a result, when people would give me directions, I often would not pay much attention to them, figuring that I would get lost anyway. Then I did get lost, not because I could not follow directions but because I had not paid attention. But my getting lost further convinced me that I lacked a sense of direction, and so I created a self-fulfilling prophecy for myself. I "knew" I was incompetent, so I did not try to do the tasks. Then I failed on the tasks, and my failure reinforced my sense of incompetence. The lesson I learned is that by telling ourselves we cannot do things, we often become unable to do them. One of the most important things you can have is a sense of self-efficacy—a sense that you can do what you set out to do.

When I hire people, that sense is the first thing I look for. Telling yourself you can do something does not guarantee you can do it. But telling yourself you can't do it almost certainly guarantees that you won't, because you will not even try. It is thus important not to give up on yourself.

▣ ▣ ▣ ▣ ▣ ▣ ▣

THINK FOR YOURSELF: *What are the kinds of forces in life that undermine people's belief in themselves, and how can people combat these forces?*

PUT IT INTO PRACTICE: *Do you believe in your own ability to succeed in your work? If not, what kinds of steps could you take to increase your belief in yourself, recognizing that belief has to come from within, not from without? Are you ever afraid to fail—or to succeed? How could you overcome such fears?*

Lesson 8
There Is Always Room to Grow

When I was a graduate student, Bill Estes, then a professor at Harvard, gave a colloquium at Stanford. He started it off by noting that he himself had funded the research he was going to discuss that day. People gasped. How could such a famous and well-regarded scientist fail to obtain funding for his work? Estes explained that, previously, he had had no trouble gaining funding to study memory-based phenomena. But then he submitted to his funding agency a proposal to study perception rather than the usual proposal to study memory. The reaction of the grant panel was that if Estes wanted to study memory, the field in which he had established his reputation, that decision was fine. But they were unwilling to fund him to study perception. They said that they did not know whether he could succeed in an entirely different field. Estes therefore funded himself, succeeded, and later gained fame—as well as funding—in his new area of endeavor. Only through his willingness to grow and escape pigeonholing was he able to turn to a whole new field of creative endeavor.

For most people, independence is something they grow into. For example, in their first year of graduate school, students may hew rather closely to their adviser's line of research. But as the years go by, they should find themselves becoming more and more independent. If they don't, they have to ask themselves why they are not growing—is it their adviser or is it their own fear of going beyond their adviser's research program?

I had an experience similar to Bill Estes's. When I first started to study love, some people thought I was nuts. They wondered what was the matter with me. Had I lost my scientific gravitas? Did I now want to be a TV personality? In fact, I just wanted to understand a phenomenon that, at that point in my life, seemed to be eluding me. Today, some of my most highly cited work is in the area of love. But the study of love did not, at the time, fit with the way people perceived me.

It doesn't end. When I recently left administration to return to being a professor, some of my colleagues wondered whether I could ever seriously be a professor again. They had me pigeonholed as an administrator. How could I possibly teach and do research again?

There will be many attempts to pigeonhole you. Some attempts, other people will make. But other attempts, you yourself will make. You tell yourself that you can do certain things but not others. Bill Estes was willing to go beyond such pigeonholing and, relatively late in his career, start a new area of research. He could do it. So can you.

THINK FOR YOURSELF: *What motivates people to pigeonhole each other?*

PUT IT INTO PRACTICE: *Do you study the issues you want or the ones others want you to, or think you should, study? How can you better become your own person rather than a person who is pigeonholed by others—or by yourself?*

Lesson 9
Don't Take Yourself too Seriously

When I was younger, I was determined never to become dead weight in my department. I even asked my students, if I ever did become dead weight, to throw me out my office window. I did not want to become an embarrassment to others, but most of all, to myself.

I remember going through an exercise of trying to figure out what the faculty members whom I considered to be dead weight had in common. I finally figured it out: What they had in common was that they all took themselves very, very seriously. They thought that they had found "truth" somewhere along the line, and they therefore stopped growing. Such people become ponderous, overly serious, and just downright boring. They are mentally moribund but seem to be the only ones not to know it. Often, unfortunately, they can be in positions of power and can make life miserable for everyone, not just for themselves. You may not be able to change them. But you can make yourself who you want to be. Don't become a crashing bore. Realize that it is important to maintain a sense of humor, most of all, about yourself.

People who take themselves and their work too seriously also often stop being creative. The reason is that if they think they have found "the answer," they have little incentive to move forward. After all, they "know" the answer. In my own career, I've never "known" any answers, really. Scientific theories and research are always incomplete. As soon as

I think I've found the final truth, it will be time for me to retire. At that point, I'll have nothing to contribute. And I hope I never reach that point!

THINK FOR YOURSELF: *Are people who take themselves too seriously less creative because they cannot imagine thinking of themselves and their ideas in new ways?*

PUT IT INTO PRACTICE: *Do you think you have any final answers in your work? If so, what would final answers mean, anyway? What other questions could you ask for which you do not have such (probably false) certainty?*

Lesson 10
Learn When It Is Time to Make Gracious Exits

Just as it is important in life to know when to enter a situation, so also is it important to learn when to leave. There are many situations in which a gracious exit is important.

Say you are in a question or discussion session. Say you make a point. Then someone else responds. Then you respond. Then they respond. Such exchanges can go on well beyond the point at which anyone is learning anything if neither party to the exchange is able to leave well enough alone. There comes a point when it is time to stop such exchanges.

I remember an exchange in a journal between scholars that I observed when I was young. Professor X wrote an article. Professor Y responded. Professor X responded to Professor Y's response. Then Professor Y responded to Professor X's response. I think it would have gone on forever had not the journal editor declared the exchange over. By that point, I doubt anyone besides the two antagonists still was interested in the exchange.

One of the most painful kinds of examples of "no exit" is the blabbermouth in a symposium who seems to believe that he or she has a direct pipeline to God and that the audience will be deprived of divine truth unless he or she keeps talking. Meanwhile, others who follow that person in the symposium are stewing in their chairs, watching their time evaporate. It has happened to me many times. A motormouth gets up and seems unable to shut up. Whether they are saying something worthwhile seems to be irrelevant. The person just loves the sound of his or her own voice and cannot seem to stop listening to it. It is the responsibility of symposium moderators to shut such people up, but often they fail to do their job, to everyone's disappointment—except the motormouth's.

Sometimes you need to make a gracious exit after you give a talk. A question-and-answer period starts. Then you discover, to your horror, that there is no moderator to stop it, or that the moderator is unwilling to stop it. Sometimes you just have to say, "I'd be glad to answer one more question," because if you don't, possibly no one else will take responsibility for ending the session.

Perhaps the most important decision about a gracious exit comes at the end of a career. When do you "call it a day" and decide to retire? I never thought much about this issue when I was younger, but I have thought about it more and more as I have grown older. On the one hand, I've seen some individuals retire when they still seemed to have a lot to contribute. On the other hand, I've seen individuals go on, and embarrass themselves and others. They are over the hill, and usually everyone knows it except them. I personally believe it is important to exit with your dignity intact. It probably behooves us all to seek sincere advice from others because it may be so difficult for us to know when the time has come to move on.

So here is a little not-so-secret fact: As I work on the second edition of this book, I am 65 years old. In years past, I would have been obliged to retire at the age of 65. In some countries of the world, I still would be forced to retire. I think I still have something to contribute: I'm working on many book projects and some articles. But when the time comes that I've emptied my plate, I'll declare myself done. I do not want to be one of those people who is the last to know it's time for me to move on. And hey, when that time comes, I'm not going to mope around. I have lots of projects planned for my retirement days, when those days finally come! Make the best use of your working days, and then when they draw to a close, be ready for the next exciting phase of your life!

THINK FOR YOURSELF: *Why do people stay in situations that may have been optimal for them once but that no longer are?*

PUT IT INTO PRACTICE: *How do you know when you are done with a project or with a career? Do you start making preparations for the next phase of your work before you are done with the last phase? How can you better prepare for the next phase?*

Lesson 11

It Is More Important, Ultimately, to Be Wise Than Just to Be Smart

There are many smart people in the field who are not wise. But the people who serve as the best mentors and ultimately, I believe, who contribute the most to the field, are people who are wise as well as smart. When I speak of *wisdom*, I refer to the application of intelligence and experience as mediated by values toward the achievement of a common good through a balance among your own, others', and institutional interests, over the short and long terms (Sternberg, 1998a, 2001, 2013; Sternberg, Jarvin, & Grigorenko, 2009).

Thus, wisdom is not just about maximizing one's own or someone else's self-interest but also about balancing various self-interests (intrapersonal) with the interests of others (interpersonal) and of other aspects of the context in which one lives (extrapersonal), such as one's city or country or environment. For example, suppose a scientist is deciding whether to report a colleague whom he suspects of fraud. His intrapersonal (self-) interest may be to say nothing; reporting the colleague may only immerse him in conflicts for which he has neither time nor inclination. But he may decide he owes it to other individuals in the department (interpersonal interests) and to the department as a whole and even to the field (extrapersonal interests) to report the suspicious colleague.

An implication of this view is that wisdom goes beyond just street smarts, or practical intelligence. When one applies practical intelligence, one may deliberately seek outcomes that are good for oneself and bad for others. In wisdom, one certainly may seek good ends for oneself, but one also seeks common good outcomes for others. If one's motivations are to maximize certain people's interests and minimize other people's, wisdom is not involved. In wisdom, one seeks a common good, realizing that this common good may be better for some than for others. An evil genius may be academically intelligent; he may be practically intelligent; but he or she cannot be wise.

Problems requiring wisdom always involve at least some element of each of intrapersonal, interpersonal, and extrapersonal interests. For example, one might decide that it is wise to take a particular teaching position, a decision that seemingly involves only one person. But many people are typically affected by an individual's decision to take a job—significant others, children, perhaps parents and friends. And the decision always has to be made in the context of the whole range of available options.

What kinds of considerations might be included under each of the three kinds of interests? Intrapersonal interests might include the desire to enhance one's popularity or prestige, to make more money, to learn more, to increase one's spiritual well-being, to increase one's power, and so forth. Interpersonal interests might be quite similar, except as they apply to other people rather than oneself. Extrapersonal interests might include contributing to the welfare of one's school, helping one's community, contributing to the well-being of one's country, serving God, and so forth. Different people balance these interests in different ways. At one extreme, a malevolent dictator might emphasize his or her own personal power and wealth; at the other extreme, a saint might emphasize only serving others and God.

Wisdom involves balancing not only the three kinds of interests but also three possible courses of action in response to this balancing: adaptation of oneself or others to existing environments, shaping of environments to render them more compatible with oneself or others, and selection of new environments. In *adaptation*, the individual tries to find ways to conform to the existing environment that forms his or her context. Sometimes adaptation is the best course of action under a given set of circumstances. But typically one seeks a balance between adaptation and

33

shaping, or realizing that fit to an environment requires changing not only oneself but also the environment. If an individual finds it impossible or at least implausible to attain such a fit, he or she may decide to *select* a new environment altogether, leaving, for example, a job, a community, a marriage, or whatever.

It is easy to point to examples of people who are (or were) quite intelligent but, in key respects, unwise. Some are psychologists. A department chair who runs a department for his or her own benefit or for the benefit of the area of psychology from which he or she comes is unwise. A researcher who fabricates data or a teacher who comes to class unprepared: Each is failing to take into account the interests of others.

I can find some examples of less-than-wise behavior in my own repertoire. When I was younger, I sometimes criticized opponents of my positions in a manner that I thought was clever, but it was also snide. When I was 25, I once blew a job interview because I gave a snide answer to a questioner. I did not realize at the time he was chair of the search committee. Oops! This way of criticizing him was unwise because it did not convince him that I had a better way of seeing things than they did, but rather, just antagonized him. Being snide or aggressive in one's critiques is an ineffective way of convincing people to see one's point of view.

THINK FOR YOURSELF: *What does it mean for you to "make a contribution to the world"?*

PUT IT INTO PRACTICE: *Do you seriously take into account the interests of others beside yourself? If not, why not? How could you change yourself to be wiser and more caring in your dealings with others?*

Lesson 12
Avoid the Major Pitfalls of the Foolish

Radovan Karadzic, accused of war crimes committed in Bosnia, is, if anything, well-educated. He is a medical doctor, a psychiatrist, in fact. Unfortunately, he is not alone among war criminals in his attainment of impressive educational credentials: Many top-ranking Nazis were highly educated, possessing doctoral degrees of various kinds. Similarly, today's most frightening terrorist is not an uneducated young male yanked off the streets but, instead, a well-educated, carefully trained individual bent on destruction.

Traditional education, and the intellectual and academic skills it provides, furnishes little protection against evil-doing or, for that matter, plain foolishness. The United States has had some very well-educated politicians and even presidents whose foolishness in their lives has cost them and their reputations dearly. Corporate and government scandals have made clear that the shenanigans of the well-educated apply to business as well as politics, and those of us who reside in the groves of academe know that foolishness can be found there as well.

At one point, I edited a book, *Why Smart People Can Be So Stupid* (Sternberg, 2002c), in which scholars who specialize in the study of human intelligence analyzed why it is that smart people can do such stupid things. My own view is that smart and well-educated people, precisely because they are so skilled, often are particularly susceptible to the following six fallacies (Sternberg, 2008):

- the *"what-me-worry" fallacy*, named after an expression used by *MAD* magazine's Alfred E. Neuman, whereby they believe that they are so smart that whatever they do will work out all right;
- the *egocentrism fallacy*, whereby they come to believe that the world revolves, or at least should revolve, around them. They then act in ways that benefit them, regardless of what the effects may be on other people;
- the *omniscience fallacy*, whereby they come to believe that they know all there is to know and therefore do not have to listen to the advice and counsel of others;
- the *omnipotence fallacy*, whereby they come to believe that their brains and education somehow make them all-powerful;
- the *invulnerability fallacy*, whereby they come to believe not only that they can do what they want but also that others will never be clever enough to figure out what they have done or, even if others do figure it out, to get back at them; and
- the *ethical-disengagement fallacy*, whereby they come to believe that ethics are important for other people, but not for them.

The high and mighty often have spectacular rises, followed by spectacular falls, because they succumb to those fallacies. Numerous examples abound—in recent times, the corruption investigation of many of the top officials of the World Cup in soccer (who worked for an organization called FIFA) comes to mind. Some very smart people did some very foolish things. What were these people thinking when they did what they did? According to the present view, they were thinking something like that they were omniscient, omnipotent, and invulnerable, and they were thinking largely, or even entirely, of themselves as opposed to others.

It once was thought, and many people still believe, that intelligence and education would alleviate human cruelty, but history does not confirm this supposition. During the 20th century, IQs increased by an average of about 9 points per generation, although one could not detect this increase simply from looking at the standardized test scores because the tests were renormed every so often to bring the mean IQ back to 100 (Flynn, 2012). This increase was essentially worldwide and was probably due in part to better education. But the 20th century also saw historic levels of massacres and genocides, not just in Nazi-occupied Europe but also in Bosnia, Rwanda, Burundi, Cambodia, Russia, and many other places. So whatever concomitants occur with increased intelligence, wisdom does not necessarily appear to be one of them. Indeed, focusing exclusively on the development of academic skills may take time away from activities that might help to develop wisdom. Academic skills are important, of course, but they are not all-important. As the example of Karadzic shows, some of the most highly intelligent and educated people use their skills cynically to foment hate and violence. We need to develop wisdom and also to avoid the four fallacies of foolishness that can ruin anyone's career.

One would like to believe that training in psychology would somehow prevent psychologists from being foolish. After all, their training is in understanding human nature. Perhaps such training does make them quicker to spot foolishness in others. But I've seen no evidence in my career that the training makes one iota of difference in terms of psychologists' own lives. Psychologists can compete with anyone for foolish acts.

▣ ▣ ▣ ▣ ▣ ▣ ▣

THINK FOR YOURSELF: *Does intelligence provide any protection at all against foolish behavior? Why or why not?*

PUT IT INTO PRACTICE: *How have you, in your career, acted in foolish ways? Have you ever believed that because you are reasonably smart, you are immune from acting foolishly? How might you avoid acting foolishly in the future?*

Lesson 13
Reinvent Yourself on a Periodic Basis

When I was a teenager, I observed that some vocalists seemed to have careers that went on and on, and others had careers that came and went like a fleeting drumbeat. Barbra Streisand has been singing forever, but have you heard any Paul Anka songs lately? What's the difference?

I believe that the difference is in the two groups of musical artists' skills in reinventing themselves. Some musical artists keep inventing new acts. In recent years, Paul McCartney and Mick Jagger have been examples. But Juice Newton, a soft-rock vocalist who experienced a brief fling with stardom, has not had so many new acts. Among visual artists, Pablo Picasso was among the best in reinventing himself.

Scientists are no different from artists in this regard. Some of the greatest scientists of the past 50 years—Richard Nisbett, Daniel Schacter, Elizabeth Loftus, Shelley Taylor, for example—have each had what seem to be many careers rather than just a single one. Nisbett, for example, has studied weight control, human inference processes, teaching statistical thinking, honor and violence, and cross-cultural cognition, among many other things. As a result, his career has never gone stale. At the same time, I have seen many scientists who essentially had one idea and were unable to move beyond it. They either tried to reinvent themselves and failed to do so or, more likely, never even tried. They became mired in their own bog. Don't let it happen to you.

Psychology 101½: The Unspoken Rules for Success in Academia, Second Edition, by R. J. Sternberg
Copyright © 2017 by the American Psychological Association. All rights reserved.

In my own career, I started off studying intelligence, then expanded to the study of love, and then to creativity, wisdom, leadership, and ethics. At one point, I entered administration, only later to return to full-time teaching and research. Change is frightening at times, but it is what keeps you fresh, or at least from going stale.

Teaching also requires reinvention. When I started out, most professors used either straight lecture or lecture plus a blackboard. Today, there are many different ways of teaching, using PowerPoint, clickers, websites, shared-access documents, and the like. The teaching of the late 1970s would seem very dated today.

It may sound like reinvention is something you only do in mid- or late career. I actually reinvented myself after my first year of graduate school. I spent my first year in graduate school studying a somewhat esoteric aspect of memory. It was fun, but it wasn't me. And it wasn't what I envisioned myself doing. By my second year of graduate school, I was studying human intelligence, which *was* me! The point is that reinvention can occur at any time in your career, from the very beginning to the very end.

▣ ▣ ▣ ▣ ▣ ▣ ▣

THINK FOR YOURSELF: *How can people prevent themselves from getting out of date?*

PUT IT INTO PRACTICE: *Are you willing to try new things? Do you ask yourself whether you are still interested in what you are doing? Do you know why you are doing what you are doing?*

Lesson 14
Practice What You Preach

I learned this lesson from a set of professional colleagues with whom I attended a meeting on psychology and education in Hong Kong. The meeting I attended was on psychology and education, in general, but an important focus of it was on the value of letting people learn from mistakes (one of the lessons in this book). Too often, teachers inadvertently disempower students who make mistakes, with the result that students become afraid to make them. They thereby lose the opportunity to learn from their mistakes.

During one of the early talks at the meeting, a relatively well-known speaker was giving a lecture, and I was only half-listening because my mind was also engaged in thinking about something else. But I was attentive enough to catch the speaker in a major blooper—or so I thought. After he finished his talk, I raised my hand, prepared to deal the coup de grace to what to me seemed to be a pathetic line of argument. He called on me, and I spoke my mind forcefully but nicely. After I spoke, the room was so quiet that one could have heard a pin drop. I found myself wondering why the room was so quiet. At that point, one of my former advisers, who just happened to be in the audience, boomed out something like, "The reason no one is saying anything, Bob, is because he never said that. You totally misunderstood his point." I have rarely been so embarrassed. I wished a trap door would open in the floor and that I could fall through it. But no trap door opened up. And so I had to spend the rest of the meeting wearing what seemed to be an invisible but nonetheless notable badge of shame.

For the rest of the meeting, people treated me like a pariah. They looked at me and I felt they were thinking to themselves, "There goes the dummy!" If only it had been the last rather than the first day of the meeting, but no such luck.

Perhaps unfortunately for the conference organizers, they had invited me to present the final talk at the conference. I had prepared a set of remarks on the talks, but when I started my final talk, I put aside my notes and made some extemporaneous remarks. I started off by saying that, at the beginning of the conference, I had put my foot in my mouth and made a damn fool of myself in the process. After all, I had made what turned out to be in all likelihood the most off-base remark of the entire conference. But I also pointed something else out.

A major theme of the conference was the importance of learning from one's mistakes. Everyone seemed to believe it was important and preached the importance of teaching it to students. But look what had happened to (poor old) me! I had made a mistake, and afterward had been treated like something of a pariah. I said that the whole experience had been pretty painful but that I was lucky in many ways because I was in a conference far from home base and eventually would leave it to go back home. Also, I was well into my 40s at the time and a full professor, so I had a series of decent accomplishments on which I could fall back. For me, it was not ego shattering.

Suppose, though, that the same thing had happened to a younger person, one who was just starting out and did not have much of a track record yet. And suppose, worse, it happened on the individual's home base. How quickly would he or she get over the mistake? And would not the person learn the very opposite of what the conference attendees were preaching, namely, the value of letting people learn from their mistakes? So here we were preaching but not practicing what we preach. Of course, I do not wish to imply that I always live up to this lesson either. I often tell students to think before they speak. The whole event never would have taken place if I had followed my own advice. We all need to do better at practicing what we preach.

I very recently found myself having made an unfortunate mistake. I had been coediting a book with a very long list of contributors. Unfortunately, one of the people who needed to be invited to contribute to the book had inadvertently been left off the invitation list. I asked myself whether to tell the contributors that I had made a mistake. As it happened, at the same time I was reflecting on this issue, I was teaching an ethics course. You can't teach about ethics and then act unethically! I told the contributors about the mistake—and they were very understanding. I also told the potential contributor what had happened, and she agreed to contribute and was pleased to have been asked. It's much easier to tell others to do something than it is to do it ourselves. For this reason, we need continually to be watching our own behavior to ensure that we do what we tell others to do. If we fail to do so, others quickly come to perceive us as empty windbags—as people who say one thing but do another. The result is that very soon they stop taking us seriously. If we want to be taken seriously, we need to not only talk the talk but also walk the walk. Do not think that hypocrisy will go unnoticed. If you act hypocritically, you may or may not notice it. Other people almost certainly will.

◻ ◻ ◻ ◻ ◻ ◻ ◻

THINK FOR YOURSELF: *What are some of the reasons people sometimes don't practice what they preach? How could they change themselves?*

PUT IT INTO PRACTICE: *Do you learn from your mistakes, or do you keep making the same mistakes again and again? How might you better learn from the errors you make?*

Lesson 15
Accept Losses Graciously

When it comes to lost battles, I'm a pro. I have had articles turned down, grants denied, proposals to the department unceremoniously rejected, and so on. During the course of a career, you inevitably win some and lose some. People will judge you as much by the grace with which you handle losses as by the grace with which you accept wins.

There are plenty of sore losers in this business. They just cannot accept a loss. I once was the editor of a book-review journal, *Contemporary Psychology: APA Review of Books*. The journal, now published in electronic form as PsycCRITIQUES, cannot review every book that is published. Many books are reviewed, but the editorial board decides not to review others. If a book is not reviewed, it is far from the end of the world. The influence of a book is not determined by whether it is reviewed in any single journal. Scholars generally prefer that their books be reviewed by the journal but recognize that some may not be.

There is a scholar who wrote a book many, many years ago. For whatever reason, the editorial board at the time decided not to review the book. The author wrote appeal letters not only to the editor but also to practically every official of any stature in the American Psychological Association (APA). When that did not work, he did not give up. He has continued to write over the years, so that every new editor of the journal and new president of APA can be assured of receiving a letter from this individual, complaining about the treatment he received many years ago and demanding that his book be reviewed. This is a man who cannot accept even a minor defeat graciously.

More recently, in my editorship of *Perspectives on Psychological Science*, an author wrote to me and said that he had had an article accepted with revisions by a previous editor but that the editor then retracted the acceptance when he took too long to revise the article. Would I now publish the article? I was sympathetic until I found out from the previous editor that the author had lied: His article had never been accepted. This is a man who cannot graciously or even honestly accept even a minor defeat. We all can do better than that.

Is it worth arguing with an editor over an editorial decision? On the one hand, it's generally not. There are plenty of journals. If one does not accept your submission, another will if the submission really is good. But there may be cases in which one would decide to argue. For example, if an editor accepted the argument of a reviewer, and the argument was truly uninformed or nonsensical, you might try appealing. I rarely do: With all the journals out there, I just don't see that it is worth my time— or the editor's. Usually, I just take the loss and "eat it."

The first time I ran for president of the APA and the first time I ran for president of the Federation of Associations in Behavioral and Brain Science, I lost. Each time I was disappointed. I congratulated the winner each time. Honestly, I felt that the people who won deserved to win more than I did. Nevertheless, each time I ran a second time and won. There's always another day, but only if you give yourself that next day.

THINK FOR YOURSELF: *What are the advantages of accepting losses graciously over becoming bitter about them?*

PUT IT INTO PRACTICE: *Are you a gracious loser? When you lose, do you reflect on why you lost and realize that, almost always, another day you will win?*

Lesson 16

Create Your Own Style of Work to Distinguish Yourself From the Rest

When you start out in a career, you are often happy to have even one idea to pursue. As you proceed through your career, chances are you will have a variety of problems available for you to tackle, and you may need to decide which one or ones are worthy of your attention. I believe that a major factor in deciding what to do is to find something that can distinguish you from the pack.

Many of us are lucky to have had good mentors. You always want to find a mentor, and preferably, more than one mentor. At first you may adopt, or at least try to adopt, the style of your mentor. But eventually you will discover that the mentor's style, however right it may be for him or her, is not right for you. You need to find your own style.

The best psychologists have a distinctive style. It cannot be hidden. Often, their work can be reviewed via masked review, in which their identity is not revealed, but it is nevertheless obvious who did the work. Why? Because they have a particular way of thinking about problems, doing research, or writing up their research that sets them apart from others.

Most academics in the sciences know how to design studies, analyze data, and write up studies. If you want to make a distinctive contribution to the field, you need to figure out something that sets you apart from

Psychology 101½: The Unspoken Rules for Success in Academia, Second Edition, by R. J. Sternberg
Copyright © 2017 by the American Psychological Association. All rights reserved.

everyone else. Often, this means coming up with your own distinctive way of doing things. There is not a one-size-fits-all way of doing things. Sometimes journal editors seem to go out of their way to homogenize the products of research, but fortunately, they do not entirely succeed. We each find our own way.

For example, my own style tends to involve coming up with some fairly large-scale theory (e.g., the theory of successful intelligence or the triangular theory of love) and then finding diverse ways of testing that theory. The research I do thus uses converging empirical operations. I tend to collaborate a lot with graduate students and postdoctoral students, but less with undergraduate students. Those are aspects of a style that works for me. Styles of work are not right or wrong. You may prefer larger theories or smaller theories, or someone else's theories, or you may prefer a biological approach of one kind or another. You may prefer working with undergraduates rather than graduate students, or you may not have graduate students available to work with. What is important is to use experience to find ways of working with which you are comfortable and that permit you to express yourself through your work.

I believe that the work an academic psychologist does can be as much an art as a science. The science, of course, is in the research. But the art is in finding a means of creative expression that sets you apart, much as an artist develops a unique style that sets himself or herself apart from other artists who might paint the same subjects. Two artists can paint the same subject but produce paintings that look very different, even though each painting reflects the same external reality. Scientists are no different. They bring their own artistic mode of expression to their science.

THINK FOR YOURSELF: *What are some of the styles of work you have observed in your mentors?*

PUT IT INTO PRACTICE: *Have you found your own distinctive style? If so, how would you characterize it? If not, how might you go about finding it, and thereby finding yourself in the process?*

Lesson 17
Don't Procrastinate

For some reason, many academics are serious procrastinators. They save things until the last minute, and even then, they often procrastinate further. My beginning an introductory psychology text is one example. But a more telling example was revising a paper I had submitted to a journal.

I wrote a paper on a certain form of reasoning called *linear-syllogistic reasoning*. Linear-syllogism problems are ones such as "John is taller than Mary. Mary is taller than Susan. Who is tallest?" I submitted the paper and, after a very long waiting period, got it back with requests for numerous major revisions.

I was very discouraged by the reviews. Although the paper was not rejected outright, the amount of work that would be needed to revise it seemed inordinate. It might take me days or even a week to revise the darn thing. So I put the paper aside, waiting for a large block of time to work on it. As the weeks went by, it became clear that the large block of time was never to come. There always seemed to be something else to do, and there were so many interruptions and disruptions of my work schedule that it became clear that the paper might be in permanent cold storage.

One day, I decided that I would just do as much of the revision as I could. To my astonishment, I finished the revision in a day. Now, I can't say many things take less time than I expect. That is not the lesson. The lesson is that by endlessly procrastinating, I had delayed publication of a major article, and for no reason. I now try not to procrastinate. All procrastination does is increase anxiety and the feeling that one cannot do whatever one is delaying. It is much better, when one is facing a forbidding task, just to get it done.

When I edit a book, I ask a variety of scholars to contribute to it. In any project, almost always one author waits until the last minute or beyond, thinking that he or she will be able to get it done before the deadline. These people are never on time for anything. I have discovered that one can wait up to a point, but after that, one is better off moving ahead with publication of the book, without the chapters of such authors. I do not ask these individuals to contribute again. Once you get a reputation as a procrastinator, you may find that few people take you seriously.

Scientific products, like refrigerated products in a supermarket, have a shelf life. A study that is of interest at a given time may, a year later, be dated or even expired. You need to get data out while they are hot. So when you do scientific work, do not procrastinate in getting it to market. If you procrastinate too long, by the time you get the work out, it may be too late.

Many years ago, I had a student who was often a good worker but was the kind of person who would never do today what he could put off until tomorrow. He did a study that was quite nice and that addressed an issue that, at the time, was quite hot in the literature. I told him that the issue on which he was working was hot but that it would not stay at the forefront forever. He finally did get around to submitting his work, but by the time he did, the field had already progressed, and his work no longer had the impact it would have had if he had submitted it in a timely fashion. Similarly, in my journal editing, I have seen authors wait too long to revise papers, and by the time they do their revisions, someone has beaten them to the punch with regard to publishing their findings. The findings are no longer new.

When all is said and done, time management is one of the most important skills to learn as an academic. You always will have too much to do. You need to figure out how you can budget your time to get it all done. You also have to figure out what is worth more or your time and what, less. Much as you might want to spend a long time working on each project, in the end, you need to decide which of your projects are worth more of your time.

Bottom line: Don't procrastinate!

THINK FOR YOURSELF: *Why do people put off for later what they can do now? What advantage do they think it gives them? Is their perception correct?*

PUT IT INTO PRACTICE: *Do you sometimes procrastinate? What would be the advantages to getting things done in a timely manner? What kinds of steps can you take to get over your tendency to procrastinate?*

Lesson 18

Capitalize on Strengths; Correct or Compensate for Weaknesses

Most people are good at something, but almost no one is good at everything. The things that you are good at can make your career; the things that you are not good at can break it. Therefore, it is important to understand your strengths and weaknesses.

Consider first the question of strengths. Some years ago, I was listening to a well-known scholar give a talk, and I whispered to the woman sitting next to me that I thought the talk was particularly wonderful and I wished I could give one like it. She looked at me and said that I was wishing for the wrong thing—that I should wish that I could give a great talk in my own fashion. I realized that she was right. I should not be trying to be great in a way that works for someone else, but rather, in a way that works for me.

Consider next the question of weaknesses. I have had wonderful mentors—primarily Endel Tulving, Gordon Bower, and Wendell Garner—and at various points of my career have wished I could have the kinds of success they had. All three have won the American Psychological Association Distinguished Scientific Contribution Award, all three are members of the National Academy of Sciences, and on and on their endless lists of scientific awards go. They fit my—as well as others'—prototypes of the

Psychology 101½: The Unspoken Rules for Success in Academia, Second Edition, by R. J. Sternberg
Copyright © 2017 by the American Psychological Association. All rights reserved.

most distinguished scientists. My work has taken me in different directions from theirs, and over the course of my career, I have had to come to terms with the fact that my career simply will not be like theirs. I think I have made good contributions, but they differ in various ways from those of my mentors.

Perhaps my contributions are more applied or, some might say, less basic scientific. Whatever they are, they are different from Tulving's, Bower's, and Garner's.

We all need to come to terms with who we are and who we can be. Successful careers are not built on emulation of mentors. They are built on figuring out our strengths and weaknesses, and then making the best contributions we can make, given those patterns.

I admire and would like to be skilled at many kinds of work—highly sophisticated mathematical and biological work, for example. But, at least up to now, they are not for me. I suspect that many a career has failed on people's trying to be something they are not. This is not to say that we cannot develop a wide range of skills. Certainly we can. But for most of us, our profile of skills is not even, and we need to pin down what we do best.

In my own career, I have found a few things I do well. I enjoy inventing theories; I write prolifically; I typically give interesting talks; I love to mentor students. So I have made these cornerstones of my career. There are things I have found I do not do well. For example, I'm not good at little details, and I have trouble sitting still in boring meetings. So I have tried to minimize the roles of these elements in my career. I have others format documents and, where possible, attend to little details. There are people who enjoy doing these things, and I enjoy working with them because they can do well what I do not do well. And I avoid committees unless I am really interested in them. When I have to serve on a committee, I have learned to pay attention and try to take an active interest. I thus have tried, where I could, to capitalize on strengths and to compensate for or correct weaknesses. It has not always worked. But it's worked well enough for me to get by.

▣ ▣ ▣ ▣ ▣ ▣ ▣

THINK FOR YOURSELF: *Do you know anyone who, instead of capitalizing on strengths, tries to capitalize on weaknesses—that is, always seems to put his or her worst foot forward? If so, what has been the result?*

PUT IT INTO PRACTICE: *What are your greatest strengths and weaknesses? How could you better capitalize on your strengths and compensate for your weaknesses?*

Lesson 19
Compare Yourself With Yourself Rather Than With Others

I believe that a serious mistake that some scholars make is to define themselves in terms of the extent that they one-up their rivals or even their colleagues. They get satisfaction not from excelling beyond their past selves but from excelling beyond their real or imagined competitors. It is always tempting to compare oneself with rivals, but it is not a constructive way to build a career.

Once, I had dinner with a famous psychologist. This is a person who by almost any objective standard has achieved a great deal of success. I was surprised to find this individual using much of the conversational time at the dinner knocking down the work of one person after another, and pointing out the ways in which his career had been superior to theirs. Today when people do this, I try to exit the conversation as quickly as possible. I don't want to reward the person for his or her negativity, and frankly, I don't want to hear the critique.

We all have to make our own decisions, but my own feeling is that I would not want to live my life building up my own self-esteem by knocking down others. I prefer to think I can do my best by challenging myself to improve on my past work, not by worrying about how I compare with others.

Still, I admit, I sometimes find myself thinking competitively. But I am disappointed in myself when I do so, and I resolve to do better. It's another example of how hard it can be to follow one's own advice—but I try.

Psychology 101½: The Unspoken Rules for Success in Academia, Second Edition, by R. J. Sternberg

When I first taught introductory psychology, I was determined to not make the mistake my own intro teacher had made. He taught the course in a way that appealed only to students who had good memories. I had a lousy memory. But I like courses that appeal to creative thinking, so I started teaching the course in a way that appealed to students who liked to think creatively. I quickly saw that the course was bombing. At first, I could not figure out why. Here I was teaching the course the way it "should" be taught, and it was not working. And then I realized what I was doing wrong. I was making exactly the same mistake my own teacher had made: I was teaching to my own strengths. But those were not necessarily the strengths of my students. To make the class a success, I had to teach to the wide variety of strengths of the students in the class, not just to my own. When I started teaching "triarchically"—to students with analytical, creative, or practical strengths (Sternberg & Grigorenko, 2007)—the course went much better. By competing with myself, and by learning from a mistake, I improved the way I taught.

At times, it's useful to compare yourself with others, for example, in looking at the characteristics of people who have been successful in job searches. But such comparisons should be aimed at improving yourself rather than at competing with others.

THINK FOR YOURSELF: *What are some of the advantages to concentrating on competing with oneself rather than with others?*

PUT IT INTO PRACTICE: *Do you tend to compare yourself with others or with yourself? If the former, would you gain more if you stuck with self-comparisons rather than comparisons with others?*

Lesson 20
Be Ethical All the Way

There are many different temptations to be dishonest in an academic career. All of them are unethical, and should be avoided at all costs (see Sternberg, 2015; Sternberg & Fiske, 2015).

The most obvious way to be dishonest in academia is to fake data. If you really are tempted to fake data, you are in the wrong field. Consider another career, such as writing fiction. There is just no room at all for fudging or faking data in science. Once it starts, where does it stop? With one data point? With one article? With all the work you ever do? If you tell yourself you will only cheat once, you are probably like the hustler who will only hustle once. Once you cross the line, you're a faker, pure and simple. Furthermore, getting away with it is harder than it looks. There are, of course, the blatant cases, such as people who use the same data points or figures and then claim that they are based on separate data collections. But even the less blatant cases can result in getting caught. People can and do request your data, and if something is wrong with the data, chances are good that people will broadcast your data fabrication.

The consequences of faking or fudging data are typically rather extreme, as in, your career is ruined. Who will want to hire you? Who will want to promote you? Who will want you as a colleague? And then, when you try to find another career, what do you tell people about why you left the first one? And if you lie, what do you do when they find out anyway? And what are you planning to do if or when the newspapers and magazines get hold of it, as they often do? I have read articles on alleged cheaters in *Science, The Chronicle of Higher Education,* and other sources mostly read by academics but also in *The New York Times* and other national newspapers.

A second way to be dishonest is to lie to the human subjects committee (which decides on whether your research is ethical) about what you will do. Maybe the human subjects committee is giving you trouble, or has given you trouble, and you figure that you can make life easier for yourself by "simplifying" your intended research procedure for them—that is, by making it look as though you are doing anything other than exactly what you are doing. This is a really bad idea. Participants sometimes complain, even with innocuous studies, and complaints trigger investigations. Or participants and others may simply talk about the study, and word gets around. If you are not doing what you said you'd do, or are doing what you did not say you'd do, that can cause trouble. Furthermore, human subjects committees can check up on you if they wish, whether or not they have reason to suspect your dishonesty.

If you are caught deviating from the approved protocol, a number of things can happen, all of them bad. The human subjects committee can and probably will shut down your research project, and they may shut down any other research projects you have, current or pending. They may also investigate past projects for deviations. If the deviation is serious, the complaint may go past the university to the funding agency. The federal government has been known to shut down all federally funded research in a university because of violations of human subjects requirements. This is bad for the university and extremely bad for you, as your colleagues will be less than thrilled that your deviation shut them down. Furthermore, if newspapers discover and publicize your deviation, then good luck dealing with the public loss of reputation. This has happened to a number of investigators, and sometimes such news articles have even made the national press. It is great to make the national press, but not for violations.

A third way to be dishonest is to tell one colleague one thing and another colleague another thing. For example, you complain to Colleague A about

Colleague X, thereby complimenting Colleague A by taking him or her into your confidence. Then you proceed to complain to Colleague X about Colleague A, reversing the process. Or perhaps you merely tell one set of facts to Colleague A and another set of facts to Colleague X. People do these little kinds of deceits all the time, assuming (probably incorrectly) that Colleagues A and X do not talk and will never talk to each other. As you do this to more and more colleagues, word will get around that you are deceitful. People then find out, sooner or later, that you are not to be trusted—not a reputation you want to have in an academic career.

A fourth way to be dishonest is with regard to feedback, such as writing a positive review of an article that you do not think is very good or writing a negative review of an article that is good. Maybe you do not like the article, but a friend wrote it and you want the friend's work to be published. Or maybe the article's conclusions agree with your theory or findings, and so you want the article published so that your views are supported. Conversely, perhaps you do not like the person who wrote the article and wish to see his or her article rejected for publication. Or you may not like what the results show and so hope to keep the results out of the literature because they disconfirm your theory. Or, even worse, maybe you hope to use the ideas yourself, and so you pan the article in the hope that it will not get published and you can do a similar study.

Giving dishonest feedback is always a bad idea. If you are the only reviewer to praise or pan an article, the editor and other reviewers may wonder whether you missed the point or what your motivation is. You risk giving yourself a bad name. And of course, it is just plain wrong.

A fifth way to be less than honest is to publish, within an article, only the manipulations that work. It is important that the field learn not only what does work but also what does not.

One of the stupidest cases of academic dishonesty I have seen in my career was with an assistant professor who formerly was at my institution (although not in psychology) when I was an undergraduate there. This individual was very vocal on campus, constantly getting himself into the local news. One thing he did not do much, however, was publish. Later, at least one reason for him not publishing much came out. It turned out that at the same time he held an appointment at my institution, he also held another full-time (and fully paid) appointment at another institution that was about an hour-and-a-half away. It turned out that he had been commuting between the two, never bothering to mention that he simultaneously held two full-time appointments. I know that my institution canned him, and I imagine the other one did the same.

Although this is the stupidest case of academic dishonesty I have witnessed, similar stupidity existed in earlier times. In the early 1900s, Cyril Burt reported exactly the same correlations for several data sets. He didn't vary the correlations even a little, which was a clear hint that his data were fabricated. And he studied IQ!

In academia, integrity is critical. There will be times when it is embarrassing to be honest, especially when you have screwed up. But it is always better to be honest than to deceive. One deception tends to lead to another, which leads to another, and eventually you can end up in much hotter water than when you started. In my experience, it is almost always the cover-up, not the original mistake, that really gets people in trouble!

One guideline that I have sometimes found to be helpful in regulating my own sense of what is ethical is that if something feels wrong, it probably is. My experience is that, when we cross the line, we usually know it, at least on some level. So keep track of your gut instincts. If something feels like it is even borderline dishonest or otherwise unethical, it probably is. Find another, better path.

The bottom line is simple: Strive for ethical behavior.

THINK FOR YOURSELF: *Why do people sometimes act unethically, even when they know such action is wrong and could cost them their careers? Is it merely about seeking short-term gains without thinking through the likelihood of long-term losses?*

Put It Into Practice: *Do you place ethical behavior as one of your top priorities, or even as your top priority, in your career? Given its importance, if you do not, how do you plan to get it to be at or near the top of your priority list?*

Lesson 21
Learn to Tolerate Ambiguity

There are periods in your life when you may try to do something in a new way. You may be trying to come up with an idea for a new experiment, an idea for a new way of teaching, or a new way of organizing courses in a department. And you may go through a period in which you don't quite have the new idea just right: You know that the old way of doing things will no longer work, but you don't yet have the new way down pat. This time can create feelings of ambiguity and hence feelings of stress. It's like an old vinyl record that is caught between two grooves. You may be tempted, in such periods, to give up on your plans to do things in a new way and to go back to your old, suboptimal, way. But you are better off tolerating the ambiguity long enough to get the new way right, even though such tolerance can be difficult.

At Stanford, I did my first-year project under Gordon Bower on a topic called negative transfer in part–whole free recall. The details of the paradigm and study are unimportant. But the project was successful. It largely resolved a puzzle in the literature. At that point, I realized that resolving a puzzle carried a disadvantage: No work was left to be done on the puzzle. So I had to find a new area in which to do research.

I had come to graduate school hoping to study intelligence, and it seemed like this was my chance to get into intelligence research. But I just could not come up with an idea I liked. I remember going to meet my

Psychology 101½: The Unspoken Rules for Success in Academia, Second Edition, by R. J. Sternberg

former undergraduate adviser, Endel Tulving, at the Center for Advanced Study in the Behavioral Sciences. I met with some of his distinguished colleagues for lunch and told them that my first-year project had gone well but that I was not sure what I wanted to do next. I remember their looking at me with what, at the time, seemed to be pity. Here I was just having finished my first year of graduate school, and I was already washed up. At that point, I thought that maybe I couldn't stand it any longer. Maybe I should just find some other problem in memory to study, which would be easier for me to do than to find a problem in intelligence. After all, I had done several studies on memory, and I should be able to find a topic for one more.

I decided instead to tolerate the discomfort of this ambiguous period. One day I was looking at materials that my wife (at the time) was using called "People Pieces." These are sketches of people, painted on tiles, that vary on four dimensions: height, girth, color, and sex. So, for example, you could have a tall, fat, blue, male. I saw a way to use the People Pieces to make analogies, and so came to me the idea for my first study in graduate school on intelligence. I tolerated the ambiguity long enough to get to where I needed to be, and thereby ended up working on problems about which I cared more rather than on problems about which I cared less.

Periods of ambiguity do not end when one is young. If anything, they may become more stressful as one gets older. After 5 years as dean of arts and sciences at Tufts University, I decided it was time to move on. I announced that I was stepping down from the deanship. I was not sure, however, what I would be moving on to. Furthermore, I was 60 years old and had a family of five to support. I was hired into another job (as a provost at Oklahoma State) a few months later, but that period of ambiguity was no easier to tolerate at 60 than at 20 or 30.

THINK FOR YOURSELF: *Why is it so hard to tolerate ambiguity? What is it that makes people so uncomfortable?*

Put It Into Practice: *Can you tolerate ambiguous and often uncomfortable situations? How can you increase your tolerance for them so that they do not create unendurable anxiety for you?*

Lesson 22
Don't Shoot Your Mouth Off—in Speaking or in Writing

I once served on a committee with a colleague who had little or no impulse control. He was constantly shooting his mouth off. The minute my colleague disagreed with someone, he said so without thinking through what he was saying. The minute he was upset with someone, he found a way to shoot a verbal barb at the person. He appeared to be very pleased with his ability to immediately attack anyone who displeased him. But he seemed to be unaware of the fact that others had long ago stopped liking him or even taking him seriously. They were so offended by his aggressive behavior that even when he made good points, people often would not listen to him.

We all know people who are very impulsive. In this case, the result was a loss of credibility. The consequences can be greater or lesser, but in my experience, they are never good. If you feel the urge to make a "killer" remark, at least think a few minutes before making it, or at minimum, count to 10! Learn to listen. Give others a chance to speak as well.

Impulsivity is a problem not only in speaking but also in writing and in various kinds of interactions with others. This is especially true for e-mail. When we are angry, it is so easy to shoot off an angry e-mail. In my experience, when I have done so, I have always regretted it very soon thereafter. The general advice is to think before you act. You'll be glad you did.

Also, don't shoot your mouth off about your research results until you know they are real. I once gave a colloquium on results that vanished when I rechecked them at the urging of an audience member. Well, that experience was embarrassing, and I never did that again. Check and double-check your work before you talk about it.

THINK FOR YOURSELF: *Why do you think that people often are so much faster to show anger than to show positive feelings?*

PUT IT INTO PRACTICE: *Has your anger sometimes gotten the better of you? How did this happen, and what price did you pay?*

Lesson 23
Control Self-Pity

There almost certainly will come times in your career when things seem to be going wrong, even horribly so. You may get one rejection after another, you may have a death in the family, you may go through a messy divorce, you may become seriously ill, your children may be in trouble, you may have legal problems, and the list goes on. Several of these things may even go wrong at once. You are not alone. In most lives, there come periods of time when nothing seems to go right.

I think that these periods are often the times that distinguish those who ultimately succeed to their levels of aspirations from those who do not. Most of us stagger or blunder through such periods and find it difficult or even impossible to work. I've been through such periods myself and wondered how I would ever get through them. But these periods do come to an end, if only you can see your way through them, and once they do, it's important to get back to work. Indeed, working on teaching, research, or administration through such periods may even help you cope. It also helps to have a close network of friends. The important thing is not to let yourself be derailed.

I must admit I have felt sorry for myself at times—maybe even a lot of times. But then I've tried to move on. Working has been a much better way of handling distress than ruminating has been. It is one thing to reflect, another to ruminate. *Reflection* is when you think about a problem and how to solve it. *Rumination* is when you turn a problem over in your mind, again and again, without any result except your becoming more and more agitated. Reflection probably helps; rumination just drives you further toward the pit of despair.

THINK FOR YOURSELF: *Is there any positive value to self-pity? If so, what? If there is positive value to self-pity, does the positive value outweigh the negative value of it?*

PUT IT INTO PRACTICE: *Do you tend to feel sorry for yourself? If you do have this tendency, can you control it? If not, are there steps you could take to move forward rather than getting stuck in self-pity?*

Lesson 24
Redefine Yourself as Often as You Need to

Some years back, a very famous cognitive psychologist came to give a talk at our institution. Before his talk began, we were sitting in my office chatting. I had just had a cognitive psychology text come out, and perhaps that was the reason the conversation turned to cognitive psychology and our roles in it. For whatever reason, he commented to me, "But you're not a cognitive psychologist anymore, Bob." I was crushed. I had been trained by Endel Tulving and then Gordon Bower, had always defined myself as a cognitive psychologist, and was very disappointed to learn that a preeminent cognitive psychologist did not consider me as one of the brethren anymore! I don't think he meant to be hurtful. I think he was just saying what he thought, and that just upset me more.

The more I thought about it, however, the less disturbed I was. My work had indeed taken me into a number of different directions, and whether or not I was a cognitive psychologist, I certainly had ceased to be a traditional cognitive psychologist. Traditional cognitive psychologists do not study love, for example.

I came to believe, and still believe, that labels can be as harmful as they are helpful. They are helpful, perhaps, in giving others a quick idea of the kinds of problems you choose to study. But they can be harmful in limiting your own definition of yourself and what you do. For example, if you define yourself as a cognitive psychologist, you may immediately decide

Psychology 101½: The Unspoken Rules for Success in Academia, Second Edition, by R. J. Sternberg
Copyright © 2017 by the American Psychological Association. All rights reserved.

that love is outside the purview of what you can study, and if you define yourself as a social psychologist, you may decide that problem solving is outside the range of phenomena you can study.

When I went into administration, I think the person who was most surprised was myself. If there was one thing I would have thought I was sure of when I was younger, it was that I never would go into administration. I ended up spending more than 13 years of life administering various entities. One never knows what the future holds!

It is important to concentrate on finding interesting problems to work on, whatever they may be, rather than to concentrate on fulfilling a set of roles specified by a label. I therefore encourage students and colleagues to follow their dreams rather than be limited by largely arbitrary labels.

THINK FOR YOURSELF: *Why do people get stuck in old ways of thinking? How can they get out of them?*

PUT IT INTO PRACTICE: *Do you define yourself or see yourself in ways that may limit your possibilities? Could you see yourself in new ways that may encourage you to try things out that otherwise you would never have experienced?*

Lesson 25
Don't Put Off Your Personal Happiness Forever:
ENJOY YOUR LIFE

There is always more to do in an academic career—a class not yet prepared for, an article not yet written. This fact creates a problem.

As an undergraduate, you may choose to work very hard so that you will get into a good graduate school. Thus, your personal life may have to be placed on the back burner. As a graduate student, you will want to get through your dissertation and get a good job, so you will need to work very hard. You may therefore decide to delay personal satisfactions. As an assistant professor, you will want promotion to associate professor, and possibly promotion to tenure, so you will need to work hard at researching and publishing. Then you will want promotion to full professor, because you will not want what for some would be the embarrassment of ending your career as an associate professor. So you continue to work hard at researching and publishing, and you continue to make personal sacrifices. And then, as a professor, you may wish to get an endowed chair. And of course there are always honors you have not yet won that are out there to be won.

My point is that if you choose to delay personal happiness and satisfaction, you may end up delaying forever. A career is important, but for most of us, it is not a full life. You need to find other things in your life. In my own case, I have studied two foreign languages as an adult, learning one to a high level of mastery and the other to a very crude first level. I have even started playing the cello again.

When I was in college, I stopped playing the cello. I had been first cellist in my high school orchestra and was dejected when, in college, it was clear that I would be, at best, in the middle of the pack. I reasoned that if I was not going to be a really good cellist, then why even bother? So I quit. Throughout most of my adulthood, I defined myself as an ex-cellist. Then, at the age of 48, I realized that I did not have to define myself as an ex-cellist and that this definition of myself was preventing me from playing again. My old cello was long gone, so I bought a new one. And I started playing and enjoying the cello again. I realized that it is not important for me to do everything really well. If I'm a rather mediocre cellist, well, so what? I'm not trying to be Yo-Yo Ma. Insisting to myself that I be the best only impeded me from doing something I enjoy.

Similarly, you need to pay attention to your significant other, your children, and others who matter in your life. Have I always been successful in doing so? No. But I have learned that in the long run, few things are more important. Someday, my work will be gone and I will be gone, and what will live on after me will be my five children and their children. They are perhaps the most important things I've had some hand in creating.

So work really hard, but don't let your work be your life. There is so much to enjoy in life and so little time in which to enjoy it. Make your life what you want it to be.

THINK FOR YOURSELF: *Why do some people keep putting off their personal lives, only later to find that they have grown too old to enjoy the things they might have done when they were younger?*

PUT IT INTO PRACTICE: *What is most important to you? How do you make sure that the way you live your life reflects the importance of whatever or whoever matters most to you?*

II
Interpersonal Relationships

Lesson 26
You Will Not Succeed in Your Relations With Everyone

During my career, I have advised well over 100 undergraduate students, graduate students, and postdoctoral students. Most of the relationships have gone smoothly. Some have not. For one reason or another, on occasion, I just did not hit it off with the student, or vice versa. On such occasions, either the student has found another mentor on his or her own initiative, or I have suggested that the student might want to look for another adviser.

When relationships with mentees have failed, I have typically felt some distress. Although I know that not all such relationships can work, I have felt partially responsible. But we all need to recognize that we cannot expect to relate effectively to everyone we encounter. Some relationships we have to write off, although sometimes with regret. I usually try hard to get relationships to work, but I also recognize that at some point, one may have to give up.

I once had a graduate-student advisee whom I felt to be quite brilliant. I tried to serve as a mentor to him, but he never seemed to listen to me. I felt as though I was a figurehead mentor, in that he always seemed to feel he knew better than I did. Eventually, I suggested he find another mentor. He needed to be advised by someone whose advice he respected, and I needed to have a student who at least listened to me, even if he disagreed. In his case, as in others, I have had to admit that the chemistry between a student and myself just was not there.

Psychology 101½: The Unspoken Rules for Success in Academia, Second Edition, by R. J. Sternberg

It is to the student's advantage to find someone with whom he or she is comfortable, and it is to my advantage not to mentor a student whom I cannot really benefit very much. So first we try to work things out, but if we just cannot do so, we both have other options.

Unfortunately, some graduate school and postdoctoral funding models make it difficult or impossible to switch mentors. For example, if a student is funded by someone's grant, that student cannot switch to another mentor without losing his or her financial support. So you may need to weigh your options carefully and think about your future prospects before making a switch.

Sometimes the failure to get along may go beyond just an individual person. You may, at some point in your life, find yourself in a department or even a college or university that just is a bad fit for you. For example, an atheist might find a religiously affiliated university uncomfortable, or someone who wants primarily to do research may find a college that emphasizes primarily teaching a bad fit. If you find your problems in getting along are not just with particular individuals but rather with lots of them, you may be in the wrong environment for yourself. My advice would be to try to get out. Although you or anyone else can adapt to new environments, you cannot be someone you're not. If you're in the wrong place, try to find the right place for you. You may want to think about finishing your studies quickly, or in another institution or, sometimes, in a different career.

I found myself in a situation where I went to a university optimistic that my fit with the people there would be superb. I had just spent several years at what I thought was a similar university. The upshot was that I was a terrible fit at the new one. My values did not correspond at all to those of many stakeholders in the institution. I tried to make things work. I got nowhere. I left. Sometimes, if you can't make things work wherever you are, you have to ask yourself whether you're in the right place!

An important aspect of life in academia is managing others, whether they are undergraduates, graduate students, or whoever. You will not necessarily get along beautifully with everyone. Make the best of it: The important thing is to get the work done, regardless of any interpersonal issues you may have with colleagues.

▣ ▣ ▣ ▣ ▣ ▣ ▣

THINK FOR YOURSELF: *What kinds of factors determine whether someone fits in a particular college or university environment?*

PUT IT INTO PRACTICE: *Do you feel a need to get along with everyone? How do you handle professional relationships in which you find that you just don't get along with someone else? What could you do better?*

Lesson 27
Don't Take Things Personally

Over the course of my career, I have published a large number of articles and books, almost all of which have been peer reviewed. Sometimes peer reviews are not very positive and may even be rather negative. And sometimes they are very negative indeed. Editors and grant-panel monitors should never send out these negative, personal attacks, but sometimes they do.

People have a tendency, especially early in a career, to take things personally. I know I did, and at times, I still do. It can be hard not to. A critique may seem to be directed at you personally and may even make ad hominem comments. But it is the rare critique that offers nothing of value—nothing that you can use to improve your work. I have learned that the best thing to do is to absolutely ignore the personal comments and hostile tone one sometimes encounters, and simply to use the comments as a basis for improving one's work. I think reviewers have, at one time or another, called me every name under the sun. As we used to say when we were kids, "Sticks and stones can break my bones, but words will never hurt me." Well, they only will if we allow them to. In essence, I try to derive something useful from a not-so-pleasant experience. And I usually can. You can, too. Concentrate on the substance and ignore the personal attacks. If the individual writing a personal attack needs psychotherapy to cope with latent hostility, that is not your problem.

Psychology 101½: The Unspoken Rules for Success in Academia, Second Edition, by R. J. Sternberg

There are other contexts in which it is important not to take things personally. For instance, in dealing with people who come from cultures or subcultures different from your own, something that you may interpret as somehow directed against you may merely reflect differences in culture.

The cultural difference may be international in origin. For example, I was once in Japan to give lectures, and had a very friendly graduate student host who seemed to be going out of her way to be accommodating. At some point in the conversation, she started talking about people who were "Aryans." I found myself taken aback. I had, from time to time, felt that some Japanese had not quite taken full responsibility for siding with the Axis powers during World War II, but I was shocked to hear that some people still believed in such racist and scientifically worthless theories as that of an Aryan race. I was ready to give her a piece of my mind when I decided that a more tactful approach was called for. I gently told her that there actually was no scientific basis for the belief in an Aryan race. Further discussion revealed that the word she had been trying to say was "alien," and that she was using it to refer to people who lived in a foreign country but who were not naturalized citizens. I realized that an expression I had almost taken as a personal affront was simply a mispronunciation caused by the fact that, in the Japanese language, there is no distinction between the "l" and "r" phonemes.

On another occasion, shortly after I arrived in Venezuela for the first time, I was speaking with a young male assistant professor. We were having a very pleasant conversation, but every so often, he would start moving closer to me. I would then discreetly back up, after which he would start moving closer again. I had a moment of panic thinking that he was coming on to me. This was the furthest thing from my mind when I had started what I had hoped would be just a pleasant professional conversation. I eventually left in a hurry. But after spending some time in Venezuela, I realized that I had misinterpreted his actions. In Venezuela, as well as some other Latin American countries, the natural distance between speakers is somewhat less than it is in the United States. We each were trying to establish what for us was the normal distance between two conversationalists. I had simply misconstrued his intentions and lost the opportunity to continue a pleasant conversation.

Cultural differences can apply not only across countries but also across parts of a single country or even across psychology departments within a country. During my early years, I gave a colloquium on my intelligence research at a well-regarded psychology department. The audience seemed to take delight in tearing me to pieces. By the time I was done with that talk, I felt like I had been through the shredder, and I felt awful because my talk seemed to have gone so horribly wrong. I later learned that it was the custom of this department to treat all their speakers in this way. They viewed their behavior as showing not that they were dismissive but, rather, that they were engaged. By not understanding the cultural context of the department, I misinterpreted the behavior of its members.

The bottom line is that you are almost always better off not taking things personally. Life is too short! Take the substance of what people say, profit from it, and move on.

THINK FOR YOURSELF: *What kinds of cultural differences might occur within a single department within a university?*

PUT IT INTO PRACTICE: *Do you take comments about your work personally? How could you deflect this personalization so as not to damage or even destroy relationships with others?*

Lesson 28
Get It in Writing

I was in my third year as a faculty member at Yale. I knew that the chances of tenure at Yale were remote, so I, like other junior faculty, was on the lookout for other job possibilities. One day, I received a call from a colleague at another institution. As I understood it, he called to offer me a job, and better, it was a job as an associate professor with tenure. All I would have to do is visit the institution where he was a faculty member, give a talk (which would be essentially pro forma), and the deal would be done.

I was ecstatic. I was getting a tenured position! I told the chair of my department what had happened, and Yale began to explore the possibility of giving me very early tenure in order to retain me. A committee was formed to consider this possibility. Now I was really ecstatic. I might get to choose between two tenured positions, one at Yale and one at the other institution!

But for whatever reason, something went wrong. I visited the institution, and no one seemed to take me seriously. My talk was not well attended, and I did not even have a formal talk with the chair. An appointment was set up with a real-estate agent, but the whole thing smelled like a farce. I returned from the trip depressed and anxious.

I then received a call from another faculty member at this university, telling me that I was mistaken: I did not have a tenure offer after all. At that point, I decided to call a faculty member I knew in the department (other than the one who initially called me), and he told me I had a "90% offer." It was all but certain. Time passed; I heard nothing. I decided to call the chair of the department, and he told me that I did not have an offer at that time but that he would get back to me. Eventually he did— to tell me that no offer would be forthcoming.

At that moment, I experienced one of the most severe humiliations I've experienced in my life. I had been "dissed" by the other institution, and Yale was considering me for tenure early on the basis of a competitive offer I did not really have! Of course, I had to tell the chair of the department, which was pretty bad. Then things went from bad to worse. He asked me to write a letter requesting that the committee considering me for tenure be disbanded. From his point of view, he was doing the sensible thing: The committee had been formed on the basis of certain information and that information now had proved to be erroneous. To me, however, his request seemed to be adding insult to injury, and I was reluctant to write such a letter.

I considered leaving Yale to go to a third institution, which seemed interested in me for a tenured position. But when I visited this third institution, I realized that all I was doing was running away from the problem. I went back to Yale, wrote the letter, and to my surprise, found that my colleagues were treating me better, rather than worse, than they had before the ugly incident. They respected the way I had handled the situation, and I established some friendships after the fiasco that might never otherwise have developed.

The upshot of this experience was that I learned an important lesson: Get it in writing. I had thought that the phone call constituted an oral offer. There is no such thing. What you do not have in writing, you simply do not have.

The mistake of believing that what one is told orally counts is not limited to young faculty. I have seen senior faculty think they have job offers they do not have or think that things promised to them orally once they accept an offer will be delivered. Sometimes the delivery fails because the chair of the department or the higher administration changes. But the bottom line is that one must have things in writing to have them at all.

▣ ▣ ▣ ▣ ▣ ▣ ▣

THINK FOR YOURSELF: *Why are oral job offers not worth a whole lot, if anything, until you have them explicitly and in writing?*

PUT IT INTO PRACTICE: *Are you relying now, in your career, on any oral commitments? Would it still be possible to get them in writing? Are you expecting any career-relevant commitments soon? Do you have a plan to get them in writing?*

Lesson 29
Don't Cover Up

At one point, a major scandal evolved among the clergy of a religious group involving sexual abuse of minors and—the point to be made here—cover-ups of the abuse. What was amazing to many people about the scandal was that those involved were supposed to be moral authorities and role models; people did not expect them to act in ways that were no different from the ways in which others might react. Latané and Darley (1970) found that divinity students were no more likely to help people in distress than were other bystanders.

Cover-ups, of course, are nothing new. Some years ago, Gary Hart, a presidential candidate, was apparently having an extramarital affair with a woman named Donna Rice. Hart not only denied the affair but also invited reporters to follow him so that they would see there was nothing to their allegations. They did follow him, and photographed him with Donna Rice on the deck of a ship. More recently, in 2015, Aaron Schock, a Congressman from Illinois, resigned. This was after attempts to cover up questionable spending on his congressional office and travel.

Many recent cases of academic fraud were spotted by and exposed by students, who are often the ones who best know the details of what is going on in a lab. Those students who reveal fraud are to be commended. Many others would have been afraid to do the right thing.

Psychology 101½: The Unspoken Rules for Success in Academia, Second Edition, by R. J. Sternberg
Copyright © 2017 by the American Psychological Association. All rights reserved.

There is no room in your career for cover-ups. As a lawyer who defended clients accused of various misappropriations once said, it is usually not the original offense but the cover-up that does people in. No one will live a life free of mistakes. You are far better off facing up to these mistakes than trying to cover for them. At times, you may need to issue an erratum to an article you have published, admit to a serious mistake in your handling of other people, or worse. Covering up is, in my experience, always a mistake. For this reason, I tell people in my research group that if an error is discovered, it is important to admit to it and face whatever consequences there are immediately, rather than to hope that it will just go away. It may go away, but the chances are greater that it will come back in a much uglier form than if you had admitted the mistake as soon as you made it. I emphasize to the members of my lab that everything we do in terms of research, finance, or practice must be completely open for inspection.

I have made my own share of mistakes; maybe more than my share. For example, a colleague and I once used a global search and replace on an article to replace one word with another, but we failed to realize that we were changing the titles of articles in the references. A colleague pointed out to us that, for some reason, one word had been replaced with the other word in the titles of these articles. If it were one article, perhaps it would not have been so bad. But it was many articles, and so the reference list was seriously flawed. We immediately sent an erratum notice to the journal. We also sent a corrected version of the article to those whom we cited in the article (and who still were living!). It was embarrassing, but it was better than the tension of hoping no one else would notice. If you make a mistake, better to admit it than to cover it up.

THINK FOR YOURSELF: *Why do cover-ups so often come back to haunt those who engage in them? Why is covering up mistakes generally a poor strategy?*

PUT IT INTO PRACTICE: *Are you living with any cover-ups now? If so, are you willing to put them behind you? How will you do so? Do you have the courage to be open in the future and take not-so-great short-term consequences, thereby avoiding even worse long-term ones?*

Lesson 30
Actively Seek Out Guidance and Feedback

Many students go to graduate school expecting to get extensive guidance and feedback, and are surprised when they do not receive it. In my experience, active guidance and feedback are often more the exception than the rule. Similarly, many junior faculty members wait a long time for the guidance that never comes. I learned fairly early in my career not to wait for others to come to me. If you want others' feedback, go to them and actively seek it. You may or may not get it, but at least you will have tried—and you will have been proactive, as you should always try to be. Don't seek feedback from just one person; seek it from multiple people. They are all likely to have at least somewhat different points of view.

I have had many great mentors—in undergraduate school, in graduate school, and as a junior faculty member. You need those mentors to help guide you in your career. The mentors need not be formal ones. Informal ones can serve you just as well. Either way, there will come times when you just don't know what your next step should be, and mentors can help guide you to that next step.

Although I am now a senior faculty member, I still actively seek out guidance and feedback. Moreover, I seek such information not just from senior colleagues but from junior colleagues as well. Sometimes, people who are less experienced than oneself see things that more experienced people do not see. Other people always see things one does not see oneself, if only one lets others comment.

I could have avoided many of the mistakes I have recounted in this book if I had sought feedback from colleagues and mentors. Often, we think we know best, we do not want to disturb others with our requests for help, or we are in a hurry to get something out. But usually we do better when we receive constructive feedback. Hence, it behooves us to ask others for suggestions and to promise to give suggestions to them when they want them.

There's one challenge we all confront when we receive feedback: Not all feedback is useful, and one cannot automatically assume it will be. Once, a colleague told me that a paper I wrote was just too ambitious— I should cut it down into several more manageable papers. I accepted that the feedback was well intended, but I also believed that if I cut the paper down into several bite-sized ones, the message would be lost. I submitted the full paper, and soon thereafter it was published.

THINK FOR YOURSELF: *Why are some people reluctant to seek feedback on their work? What are they fearing?*

PUT IT INTO PRACTICE: *Do you actively seek feedback on your work? Do you pay attention to feedback when you receive it? Do you carefully evaluate the feedback to assess how useful it is?*

Lesson 31
Avoid Defensiveness

On arriving at Stanford for graduate school, I decided to seek my new graduate adviser's feedback on a paper I had written as an undergraduate. I was quite proud of the paper and even had presented it at a professional convention in Chicago. A few days later my adviser, Gordon Bower, returned the paper. He told me he had crossed out the areas he thought were weak. I looked at the paper and was horrified to see that he had crossed out almost the entire paper, with comments to match. There was very little left of my original product.

My first reaction was to make an appointment to talk to him to tell him what a terrible mistake he had made. But I decided to think things through a bit more, and as I reflected on his comments, I began to realize that I essentially agreed with the points he had made. By dropping my defensiveness, I had given myself a learning opportunity that I otherwise would not have had.

Sometimes it's hard not to be defensive. I once received in the mail a published critique of my work that ran to almost 100 pages in length. The critique was angry, sarcastic, often ad hominem, and full of attempts at one-upmanship—or at least I saw it that way. I was surprised that it had been accepted for publication, but it had been. So I wrote a reply, and I guess I lost it. I wrote a very detailed, point-by-point refutation of the critique, defending myself against the numerous charges made in the article criticizing my work.

Psychology 101½: The Unspoken Rules for Success in Academia, Second Edition, by R. J. Sternberg
Copyright © 2017 by the American Psychological Association. All rights reserved.

The reply I wrote was reviewed, and the reviewers were less than enthusiastic about my response. They believed that it came across as defensive and boring, and that no one would be interested in reading a point-by-point rebuttal. I realized that the reviewers were right—that no purpose was being served by my replying in such a fashion. I therefore threw out most of my lengthy reply, figuring it had served a purpose of psychological catharsis for me—but little else—and wrote a reply that was more positive and more global.

Over the course of my career, I have observed that students profit in very different degrees from the environment we provide in our department, in our university, and in our center. Some seem to learn a great deal and seriously improve themselves; others improve relatively little. I think a key difference between the two groups is with regard to their relative levels of defensiveness. Some students use feedback as an opportunity to learn; others seem to learn little from the feedback they receive. I've had students start out fairly far behind who eventually advanced ahead of others, not necessarily because they were "smarter," at least in a traditional sense, but rather because they were willing to take guidance and learn in a nondefensive way. Defensiveness closes you off to growth and, really, to fulfillment of your potential. Thus, you may feel like you are helping yourself in blocking out criticisms or feelings of rejection, but the truth is that you are doing anything but helping yourself.

The need to be nondefensive does not end when one becomes a professional. Learning is a lifelong experience. People who allow themselves to profit from feedback—even painful criticism—will continue to grow and improve throughout their entire career.

THINK FOR YOURSELF: *What are the advantages of taking criticism constructively rather than taking it defensively and personally?*

Put It Into Practice: *Do you take feedback well?
If not, why not? What steps should you take to reduce
the possibility of reacting defensively to feedback
intended to help you?*

Lesson 32
Make Friends in the Field

I've had some great strokes of luck in my career. I've won a number of awards; I've become a fellow of a number of professional associations; I've been awarded 13 honorary degrees; and I have been asked to speak in countless places. On the one hand, I've probably earned at least some of these honors! On the other hand, I probably would have received few of these honors if I lacked friends in the field.

Behind every award, every fellow nomination, every honorary degree, every speaking engagement, is someone who nominated me. I may have been a good choice, but the truth of the matter is that many other people would have been good choices as well. In each case, someone chose to nominate me, when he or she could have nominated countless other deserving people. It helps to have friends who care about you, because they are the ones most likely to nominate you for things.

At the same time, it is important to remember that friendship is reciprocal. I have nominated many people for various awards. In every case, they were people I felt were eminently qualified for the award. But the truth is, many people are potentially qualified. Just as friends are more likely to nominate you than to nominate people they do not know, so you are more likely to nominate friends than people you do not know.

Friendship is not just instrumental. Academic psychology is a tough business. You need all the friends you can get, just to stay sane—people with whom to share problems, with whom to speak about things you need to get off your chest, people who mean something to you. I have often felt I would be lost without having good friends in the field.

I think one of the most important aspects of friendships with people in the field is trust. If you cannot trust someone and that person cannot trust you, that person is not your friend, no matter what other things the relationship may have going for it.

Another important aspect is commitment. A friend is someone who will stick with you when the chips are down. I have seen academia take a brutal toll on some people. But the most brutal toll of all is when their lives start falling apart and people they thought were their friends all of a sudden find it convenient to make themselves scarce. One person I know was accused—falsely, from what I can tell—of a professional misdeed. What was worse than the false accusation was the speed with which supposed friends and colleagues deserted what they thought was a sinking ship. If you want to be a true friend to a colleague, then you need to commit yourself to that colleague (see Sternberg, 1998b).

If you are still in graduate school, your friends will probably be your fellow graduate students. Chances are high that the relationships you form in graduate school will continue throughout your entire career. I am still in touch with many of the friends I made in graduate school, 40 years after leaving it.

I've been through some professionally very challenging periods in my career, including recently. I always learn something from these challenges. One of the things I have learned is who my true friends are.

THINK FOR YOURSELF: *Why are friendships in the field important? What are some potential costs of not having them?*

PUT IT INTO PRACTICE: *Are you seeking to make friends not only in your personal life but also in your professional life? If not, what more could you do to make friends among your colleagues?*

Lesson 33
Be True to Yourself and Let Others Be True to Themselves

When I was deciding on what to do for a career, I was pretty sure I wanted to be a psychologist. I was not entirely sure, though, and in my junior year of college I took a prelaw course on constitutional law and decided that, although it was interesting, it aroused no passion in me. And constitutional law was what I figured would be the most interesting aspect of the law.

Meanwhile, my mother was eager for me to attend law school. She believed, for whatever reason, that I had the right combination of attributes to be a lawyer. My older brother was studying law, and why not have two lawyers in the family? It was hard to tell my mother that I was not interested in going to law school, but I finally did talk to her.

Three years later, when I was about to receive my PhD, I had a conversation with my mother. She pointed out that the president of Rutgers University at the time had both a psychology degree and a law degree, and that I could do the same. I told my mother once again that I was not interested in a law degree.

Five years past the PhD, when I was tenured, my mother and I had another conversation. She pointed out that I had now proved to myself that I could be a successful academic psychologist and that it still was not too late to go to law school—that people went even when they were early in other kinds of careers. For the last time, I told her that I would not be going to law school. She never brought up the issue again.

Many of the students in my college graduating class did, in fact, go to law school. I have seen them from time to time at college reunions. My experience with them has been that those who went to law school because they were enthusiastic about it generally are reasonably happy with what they are doing, but those who went because it was the "right thing to do" or because they succumbed to parental or other pressures are, for the most part, quite unhappy and eagerly awaiting retirement. I have had no doubt that I did the right thing not going to law school. And I have made no effort to insist or even encourage my own children to go to law school. But life works in mysterious ways: My daughter Sara is now a law professor!

In working with my children and my students, I try to help them find what interests them, whether or not it particularly interests me. Often, their enthusiasm is infectious, and I find myself drawn into new areas of pursuit simply because I allow myself to follow my children rather than always expecting them to follow me. Even now, at the age of 65, I find that my students lead me: By letting them pursue their interests, I have acquired new interests that I might never have found had I not allowed myself to be led in those directions.

I often meet students who are pursuing a certain career interest not because it is what they want to do but because it is what their parents or other authority figures expect them to do. I always feel sorry for such students because I know that although they may do good work in that field, they almost certainly will not do great work. It is hard for people to do great work in a field that does not ignite some kind of passion in them.

Of course, taking this attitude is easier said than done. When my son Seth was young, I was heartened that he wanted to play the piano. I play the piano, and I was glad that he wanted to play too. But then he stopped practicing and ultimately quit, and I felt bad. A short time thereafter, he informed me that he had decided that he wanted to play the trumpet. I reacted very negatively, pointing out to him that he had already quit the piano and probably would quit the trumpet too.

I then found myself wondering why I had been so harsh. How could I have said such a thing? But then I quickly understood. If someone else's child wanted to play the trumpet, that was fine. But I couldn't imagine any Sternberg child playing the trumpet. It did not fit my ideal image of a

Sternberg child. I realized I was being narrow-minded and doing exactly the opposite of what I had told everyone else to do. It's one thing to talk the talk, another to walk the walk. I backpedaled, and Seth started playing the trumpet.

Eventually, he did, in fact, quit the trumpet. Finding the right thing is frustrating work! But Seth eventually did find the right thing. He went into business, working for IBM in acquisitions and divestitures of companies. Today he is a very successful entrepreneur in Silicon Valley. Is it what I would have wanted for him? Doesn't matter! The important thing is that he found what is right for him. Find what is right for you, and let others find what is right for them.

THINK FOR YOURSELF: *What are the pressures people encounter in their lives not to be true to themselves?*

PUT IT INTO PRACTICE: *Do other people try to impose their vision for your future on you? Do you try to impose your vision for others' futures on them? How can you resist the temptation either to impose or be imposed on?*

Lesson 34
When You Make a Professional Commitment, Honor It If at All Possible

I enjoy editing, and have edited many books, often in collaboration with students and other colleagues. Each edited book I undertake requires a set of authors to contribute chapters. There are some people whom I would like to ask to write but whom I do not ask because they have proven themselves to be unreliable. They say they will write, and then cop out, often at the last moment. In doing so, they show themselves not only to be unreliable but also to be lacking in consideration of others, because all authors in the book are affected if one person pulls out.

It is extremely important to meet the professional commitments you make. If you are not sure if you can meet a commitment, do not make it. If you make it, then do your best to meet it. If you absolutely cannot, then try to work out something with the person, persons, or organizations to whom you have committed yourself. Perhaps you can find someone else of equal standing to do what you said you would do, or perhaps you can work out a time schedule so that you will do what you said you would do, only a bit later. Remember, you may have good excuses, but the chances are that those to whom you have committed have heard these excuses, and many others like them, before.

I travel too darn much. I keep trying to cut back my travel schedule, but somehow it always ends up being onerous. Sometimes a planned trip

Psychology 101½: The Unspoken Rules for Success in Academia, Second Edition, by R. J. Sternberg
Copyright © 2017 by the American Psychological Association. All rights reserved.

sounds really good at the time I make the plans, but then when the time rolls around for the trip, it no longer sounds so great. Sometimes what I see are long lines and irritating security procedures at airports, time lost listening to talks in which I am not terribly interested, meetings with people whom I do not always have any great desire to meet. But if I have made the commitment, I make every effort to keep it. It is a matter of respect for those to whom I have made the commitment, but also respect for myself. I do not want to view myself as someone who says one thing and does another. I've done it at times but have always felt pretty lousy about myself afterwards.

The most memorable example in my own life was when I agreed orally to sign a textbook contract with one company, and the acquisitions editor for the textbook (the person who contracts the book) and her boss agreed to come to New Haven to have lunch with me the following week. After making this oral agreement by phone, an acquisitions editor for another company showed up at the front door of my home—literally—and persuaded me that I should sign with him. I did. He left with a signed contract. Monday morning I called the acquisitions editor who was planning to visit to tell her that I had signed with the other company, and I was truly sorry. But she and her boss had left for New Haven. I felt terrible. They arrived at my door. I gave them the bad news, and they left angry and feeling betrayed. Although my commitment had not been written, I had orally committed myself and then backed out. I felt badly at the time and still do, more than 25 years later! My mistake was not in signing with the second publisher. It was in orally (and informally) committing myself to the first publisher and then signing with the second. Although I was under great pressure to sign with one or the other publisher, I should have waited to commit myself, even orally, until I was absolutely sure that signing with the first publisher was the right thing to do. So: If you make a commitment, keep it!

I had a colleague agree to do an important task for me with respect to a journal I edit. The colleague failed to come through. He was "too busy." Who got hurt? Well, he did: It hurt his reputation. I did: I counted on the wrong person and people saw I made a mistake in judgment. The authors who were affected got hurt: They did not get the responses to which they felt they were entitled. The organization publishing the journal got hurt: People felt that they deserved better service from the publisher. In other words, when you fail to fulfill a responsibility, many different parties can be hurt as a result of your lack of responsibility.

You may choose to have a set of criteria for undertaking commitments in the first place. In that way, you will not find yourself stuck with any, or at least many, projects that you later regret having undertaken. Some guidelines you might use are whether (a) you will enjoy the project, (b) it will benefit you professionally, (c) you will meet new and interesting people, (d) you will get to know people better whom you already know, (e) the opportunity will teach you new knowledge or skills, and/or (f) the commitment is onerous. Everyone has to set up his or her own guidelines, but you need some guidelines to prevent your finding yourself with a bunch of commitments you regret having made.

There may be times when you need to break commitments. You have agreed to give a talk, but you get sick; you have agreed to do a job interview, but you are on the verge of accepting another job; you have agreed to do a task but find that you totally lack the skills to do it. When you have to break a commitment, do so as soon as possible; explain why you are breaking it; apologize; and move on.

THINK FOR YOURSELF: *When you make a commitment you are having difficulty keeping, what's the best course of action?*

PUT IT INTO PRACTICE: *What commitments are important to you? How will you make sure you keep them? How do you keep yourself from making commitments you might later find yourself unable to honor?*

Lesson 35

Give Students and Colleagues Guidance, but Allow Them the Freedom to Find Themselves

Whether you are a colleague or a mentor, you may or may not have a style or set of styles that matches the styles of the people you work with. But it is important to try to adapt yourself so that you can work with a wide variety of people. In the course of a career, you will be working in various capacities with thousands of people. Many of the things you work on will be team efforts in which collaboration is the name of the game. If you cannot collaborate successfully, you may find that you will not succeed in your endeavors to the extent you would like to. In particular, if you are a mentor, don't try to control your mentees.

I have seen advisers take very different paths with their students. My graduate adviser, Gordon Bower, allowed his students to do pretty much what they wanted (within reason). He provided guidance but did not try to control what they studied or how they studied it. The result: It would be hard to find a professor who has had a more professionally successful set of graduate students. I cannot think of any in my lifetime. I am grateful that I was fortunate enough to have been Bower's graduate student.

Other advisers try to control the topics their students study, the way they study those topics, or more likely, both. They create explanations to give to others and even to give to themselves. The real explanation, in my view, is that they are either egocentric or selfish, or both. They just can't imagine that a student could have better ideas than they do. But in my experience, students often do have better ideas. Although they have less domain knowledge, they are more flexible. So everyone pays a price: The student does not get to develop independently, and the adviser gets stuck in doing variants of the same things, over and over again. Obviously, not everyone agrees with me, and the fact that I view things this way does not make my view true! But I think one would be hard-pressed to find a highly controlling adviser who has had anywhere near the success Gordon Bower has had with his students over the years.

If you are a student, you need to set the course of your own research career, not have someone set it for you. Choose an adviser who will let you be you.

□ □ □ □ □ □ □

THINK FOR YOURSELF: *What are reasons that advisers want students to be junior versions of themselves? Are there advantages? How about disadvantages?*

PUT IT INTO PRACTICE: *Does the work you do match the way or ways you prefer to think? How could you modify what you do, or how you learn, to better fit with what you need to get done in your life?*

Lesson 36
Don't Try to Please Everyone

You will come upon times in your career when the opinions of particular other people are important to your future. Sometimes you will have to make an attempt to raise their opinion of you. In principle, there is nothing wrong with trying to make people happy. Where you go wrong is when you try to please everyone, or when you are indiscriminate in whom you try to please. At times in my life, I have tried to please certain people and later regretted it. I regretted it because I realized that there simply are some people who will never be pleased with what I do, and that the more I try to please them, the less pleased I will end up being with myself. And I have decided it is just not worth selling myself out for their sake. I remember in particular trying to please a certain faculty member whom I had been told would oppose my bid for tenure. I realized that there was no way to please him. It didn't matter what I would do: He didn't like anything I did and probably never would. So be it.

To give you a concrete example: In the field of intelligence—one of the main fields in which I work—there are fairly active disagreements over just what intelligence is. I am among those people who believe that intelligence has multiple facets that are distinct from each other. Other people in the field believe that intelligence is just one thing. I have, at times, tried to find compromise positions that would make some of these people— even the extreme ones—happy. I have found no compromise position that mollified them. And I have realized that there probably is none. We simply disagree. And it's OK to disagree.

A particularly taxing situation is when you are in an environment in which you can't seem to please anyone. It's as though you suddenly have walked into a world different from the one in which you have lived before. It's happened to me. Life is a balance of adapting oneself to new environments, shaping those environments, and selecting new environments. If you are in an environment in which no one is happy with you, you may be in the wrong environment. Consider getting out and finding an environment that is more appreciative of your talents, interests, and points of view.

THINK FOR YOURSELF: *What are the advantages of not pleasing some people?*

PUT IT INTO PRACTICE: *Do you try to please everyone? If so, why? Would you like to change yourself? How could you go about doing that?*

Lesson 37
Don't Bad-Mouth People Behind Their Backs

Whenever I hear someone bad-mouth someone else behind that person's back, it gets me very upset. First of all, it is not right. If you have something to say, you should be able to say it to the person's face. I try to say the same things to people about themselves that I say to others about them, and hope they will do the same for me. Second, bad-mouthing others invites them to do the same to you. Third, I realize that if someone I am talking to is bad-mouthing other people to me behind their backs, the chances are pretty good that the individual is doing the same thing to me behind my back. So when I hear someone bad-mouth others, I conclude that he or she is not trustworthy. There is no reason to expect the individual to treat anyone differently. Finally, if you expect that your words will not get back to the people you bad-mouth, think again. It's a losing game because sooner or later people discover the kind of person you are. Bad-mouthers are attempting self-aggrandizement at the expense of others.

Over the years, I have known quite a few bad-mouthers. They will appear to be good friends with people, and then, behind those people's backs, say things that I am sure they would never say to their faces. These folks make me very nervous. I know that if they do it to others, they will do it to me. I also practice what I preach: I avoid saying anything behind someone's back that I would not say to his or her face.

Psychology 101½: The Unspoken Rules for Success in Academia, Second Edition, by R. J. Sternberg
Copyright © 2017 by the American Psychological Association. All rights reserved.

Be especially careful about disparaging people through e-mail. E-mails have a nasty way of being forwarded. And sometimes we mistakenly send them to the wrong people—perhaps even to the person we're bad-mouthing! These days, I know more people who get themselves into trouble via e-mail and social-media postings than via other kinds of methods. Also, remember that once you send an e-mail or post on social media, it never really completely disappears, even if you think you have deleted it. You need to be really careful with what you say online!

THINK FOR YOURSELF: *What exactly are the benefits of being a bad-mouther? What does one gain? What are the costs?*

PUT IT INTO PRACTICE: *Do you bad-mouth people behind their backs? If so, are you prepared to stop? Is being a bad-mouther really who you want to be? If not, can you move on and, in the future, refrain from talking about people behind their backs?*

Lesson 38

Be Generous With Your Time, but Don't Let Others Rob You of It

Every day, I receive substantial amounts of e-mail from people I do not know. Maybe you do too. As I mention at the beginning of Lesson 6, some of the e-mails are from people who want information that easily could be gotten from reading any of a number of articles or books I have written. I have colleagues who are willing to spend a great deal of time answering such e-mails. I have decided that I am not. Although I answer the e-mails— I view it as a professional responsibility—I typically write back only briefly, suggesting they consult the appropriate published resources. I often then suggest that if, after reading the article or book, they still have questions, they write back. I realize that they may not read anything and that I may have missed an attempt to educate a member of the public on some issue that I may really care about. But I just do not view it as a good use of my time to answer individually questions that I already have answered through my writings. I also receive many e-mails from students who have questions for class papers that they have to write. Again, I reply briefly but am not willing to answer the long lists of questions I sometimes receive. To me, such demands are unreasonable and not worth much of my time. I am not saying others should feel the same way. Rather, I am saying that we each must decide which of the demands on our time are important and plan accordingly. Don't waste your time when people make unreasonable demands on your time, and do not make unreasonable demands on the time of others.

Psychology 101½: The Unspoken Rules for Success in Academia, Second Edition, by R. J. Sternberg
Copyright © 2017 by the American Psychological Association. All rights reserved.

Many of the opportunities I have had in my life have come from giving at least somewhat generously of my time. I once received a call from someone I did not know, offering for me to do some vague kind of project overseas. I was pretty busy. It sounded like a distraction from what interested me most. I felt like hanging up and moving on with my work. But I listened; I had several more conversations. I ended up with what I now view as perhaps the most interesting research program in my career.

THINK FOR YOURSELF: *What are costs of being either too stingy or too generous with your time?*

PUT IT INTO PRACTICE: *Do you allocate your time and energy in ways that serve your goals? Are you generous with your time without being foolish in lending it out to people who really should know better than to make excessive demands? If so, is it time to change?*

Lesson 39
Be Open and Be Straight

On the one hand, it makes sense to talk to people in a kind and humane way. I strongly believe that there is no place for belittling or demeaning one's students, colleagues, or friends. At the same time, some people are afraid to say what they think. In my experience, the results are usually unfavorable. It is better to be open and straight.

I once had an assistant who seemed continually to be afraid to speak her mind. We would go through relatively long periods in which, no matter how she perceived what I said to her, she would respond graciously and even meekly. And then, once a year or so, she would just explode. The explosion usually was set off by something minor and would seem to be like an explosion of a powder keg. She had built up resentment in successive increments, and when the resentment reached some criterion level, the explosion would come.

There are several problems with this mode of relating. One is that problems that could have been solved weren't because she never shared with me what she perceived to be a problem. A second is that it is fundamentally not honest. She was thinking one thing and saying another. And a third problem is that when the explosion did come, little was resolved. She would be so angry that any kind of meaningful discussion was very difficult to have. We both would have been much better off if, when she had something to say, she had simply said it.

One form of not being straight is keeping inside you the issues you have with another person. Another form is being duplicitous. Years ago, I collaborated with someone on a research project. The project went well. Then, when we were discussing order of authorship (I thought she should be first author), the collaborator stunned me by saying that she thought Professor X should be first author. What was stunning was that I had not even known that Professor X had been involved in the project. So all of a sudden I was discovering a silent partner. I rejected this request (which was posed almost as a demand) and talked to Professor X, who said he should not, in fact, be listed as a coauthor. I don't know whether it was my outrage or whether it was that he thought that the collaborator was off base. But this kind of duplicity almost certainly will spoil any relationship.

Being open with people can be painful at times, but in the long run it generally pays off. And I think people respect you more for it. Can I guarantee that there will never be people who will hold openness against you? Of course not. There are people who will hold your honesty against you. But then the question is, do you want to be like them, or to let them determine your behavior?

I have discovered that cultures and even subcultures differ with regard to the amount of openness they expect and promote. So you probably want to try to find an environment that matches the level of openness you are prepared to offer and receive. I once was in an environment where nobody seemed to be open about anything. Everything seemed to be a big secret. I left. It may have worked for the people there. It sure didn't work for me.

In being open with people, remember that there is always room for tact. You can say what you have to say in a nice way. But do your colleagues and yourself a favor: Say it. Don't give them the job of having to read your mind. With an adviser, you have to be especially tactful. But if you cannot speak to them about what's on your mind, you are probably with the wrong adviser.

THINK FOR YOURSELF: *Why are people often afraid to say what they think?*

PUT IT INTO PRACTICE: *Are you open with other people?*
If not, why not? In any case, is the amount of openness
encouraged or even allowed by the environment you
are in consistent with your personal preferences?
If not, would you consider moving on to an environment
that is a better fit to who you are?

Lesson 40
Think Before You Speak

In almost any group, there seems to be at least one individual who is the motormouth—the person who always has something to say, and says it at length, regardless of whether it is worth saying or not. Such windbags often lose their credibility, because they are readily recognized as people who shoot off their mouths. But they can sometimes destroy themselves and others through their impulsivity.

I once consulted for an individual who was in a very high position in a company. At one point, the position above him became available, and he was one of the candidates. He was very hopeful that he would get it.

One day he received a telephone call from the CEO telling him that he did not, in fact, get the position. Extremely distressed, he mouthed off to the CEO, telling him that it was a bad choice that the CEO would later regret. In fact, the person who later had cause for regret was the motormouth. He not only did not get the promotion, within short order he lost the job he had. It really pays to think before you speak!

In many groups, one person or another seems to fill the role of the person who shoots his or her mouth off and seems to need to keep talking and talking. Such people are almost never the ones called on to take critical roles in the group. They may have something to contribute, but they undermine their own credibility by their impulsive expatiations.

Psychology 101½: The Unspoken Rules for Success in Academia, Second Edition, by R. J. Sternberg
Copyright © 2017 by the American Psychological Association. All rights reserved.

I admit I've said some pretty stupid things in my life. They usually were said when I just spouted them out without first thinking them through. E-mail is the worst. Once you say something there, you can't take it back. Once you send an e-mail, you can't recall it without the recipient seeing it. Do yourself a favor: Think before you speak! And while you're at it, think before you hit the Send button on that e-mail. The next time you are angry and ready to click Send, just wait. Wait until tomorrow—or at least wait an hour, but wait.

THINK FOR YOURSELF: *What signs can you observe in yourself that you are about to say something impulsively that you may later come to regret?*

PUT IT INTO PRACTICE: *Do you think before you speak? If so, how can you avoid doing so again?*

Lesson 41
Networking Matters—
Up to a Point

It is sometimes said that "it's not what you know, it's who you know." That statement is, in my experience, false. What you know does matter. At the same time, who you know matters, too. When I was president of the American Psychological Association, I was involved directly or indirectly in many assignments of people to task forces, committees, and boards. No doubt, people who are known to the decision makers are more likely to be chosen. Similarly, in getting jobs, having some kind of personal contact or connection can make a difference in the result. Having genuine friendships, as mentioned earlier, is even better.

At the same time, some people try to use networking as a substitute for substance. In my experience, this strategy rarely pans out. It may work over the short term, but eventually people realize that you are an empty shell. And people often will resent that you attempt to substitute substance with show. Ideally, you will combine substance with a broad and deep network of associates.

I know one individual who seems to manage to be on every committee around. She seems to be the ultimate networker and hence is asked to serve, again and again. But when I think about what the person has to show for having been on all these committees, it is hard to say, other than multiple lines on a vita. Networking is no substitute for substance. You want to develop a network not in place of substantive contributions but rather so that others can appreciate the substantive contributions you make. Networking is very important and needs to be developed in addition to, rather than instead of, substantive contributions.

I'm not the greatest networker. It's probably hurt me in my career. So by all means, pay attention to creating and maintaining networks. But never let those networks substitute for your paying attention to the substance of what you need to get done!

THINK FOR YOURSELF: *How do you know whether the network you are establishing is right for your career goals?*

PUT IT INTO PRACTICE: *Could you pay more attention to establishing and maintaining your networks? What concrete steps could you take now to enhance your networking and thus your connection with other people in your field?*

Lesson 42
Distinguish Between More and Less Important Battles

In departmental meetings, in various board meetings, and in almost any other interaction I have with anyone, discord sometimes arises. It is important to distinguish the battles from the wars. Some issues are worth fighting for and fighting for hard; others are not. It is important to learn early in your career which are which, and to act accordingly.

When I was a graduate student, I made a fuss about having a final examination in a particular course. I thought it was inappropriate, given the kind of course it was. I actually got into an argument with the professor. Was I right? Maybe, maybe not. Was it worth arguing about? No way!

One of the most precious commodities in academia is space. I have been to many universities in which faculty members were slugging it out for space; I have not been to many where faculty members had more space than they could use (actually none, to be exact). Once upon a time, I was engaged in a space battle. Some years ago, when I was at Yale, my colleagues and I acquired for what was then our Center for the Psychology of Abilities, Competencies, and Expertise (PACE Center) a wonderful old house on the northern edge of the Yale campus. This historic house, built at the turn of the century, actually had two U.S. presidents sleep in it (Taft and T. Roosevelt, who spent a night there ironing out differences they had) and had a very distinguished history. The only problem is that we did not acquire all the rooms in the house for the PACE Center. Some of the rooms were then allocated to visitors in international relations.

Psychology 101½: The Unspoken Rules for Success in Academia, Second Edition, by R. J. Sternberg
Copyright © 2017 by the American Psychological Association. All rights reserved.

After protracted and difficult negotiations, we acquired more space from the university—across the street. So the plan was that our group would be split up and that the visiting faculty in international relations would continue to occupy space in the house. We made numerous attempts to swap space and to do everything we could so that we could stay together. Every time we thought we had the space swap arranged, it fell through. Finally, we decided to occupy the space across the street. It was not our ideal. But it was clear that we had lost this battle, plain and simple. It just was not worth fighting anymore. So we admitted defeat and moved on. Sometimes in one's career, one has to decide which battles really matter and are worth pursuing to the end, and which ones aren't. We decided that this one wasn't.

In my career, there has been one battle that, unlike the one over space, has been particularly important to me. It is the battle to free this nation from the yoke of standardized tests that often are claimed to reveal much more about students than they actually do. In my view, the tests have become a tyranny, preventing many individuals from reaching their potential. How often, in one's adult life, do one's answers to the questions on these tests make a bit of difference? Probably never or almost never, and yet I feel we treat the tests with far greater respect than they deserve. I realize many others disagree with me. Each person is entitled to his or her own opinion. But I'm continuing to fight the battle not against any use of these tests, but against their overuse. So far, I'm losing. But I'm not giving up! At this time, my psychologist wife and I are trying to form an enterprise that will make better college admissions assessments to colleges that want to use them. These assessments measure not just analytical skills but also creative, practical, and wisdom-based ones, as well as passion and writing skills. Will we succeed? I don't know, but we have to try.

THINK FOR YOURSELF: *How does one decide which battles are worth fighting?*

PUT IT INTO PRACTICE: *Have you carefully selected what battles are worth fighting, both past and present? When you find ones that are worth your time and energy, how do you keep yourself going in the face of the occasional but inevitable reversal?*

Lesson 43
Don't Hold Grudges

Early in my career, I wrote a book that was, at the time, very important to me. It was the book that I hoped would launch my professional career. The publisher sought external reviews before publishing it and, as I recall, two were quite positive. A third one was devastatingly negative. The reviewer wrote 17 single-spaced pages slamming the book and saying, in essence, that the publisher would be crazy to publish it. From what I heard, I was not the first person to be on the receiving end of such treatment from this individual. I was lucky: The publisher chose to disregard the review, suggesting only that I take from it what I thought would be helpful to me, and published the book. The book later became a citation classic of the Institute of Scientific Information.

Although the review was anonymous, it was pretty obvious who wrote it. I was extremely distressed at the time. I was distressed that I was so early in my career and had already managed to make an enemy. Over the years, I have had many interactions with this individual, including reviewing his papers and books. I had a choice of whether to hold a grudge or to let go of what had happened. I decided to let go. There was no benefit either to me or to the individual in my holding a grudge. Over the years, we have even become friends, although perhaps not close friends. I have gained quite a bit from my interactions with this individual, knowledge that would have been lost to me had I held a grudge. I believed that, whatever the person's flaws, there was a basis for a relationship.

I have been on the receiving end of a grudge, however. Once I noticed that a colleague was acting strangely toward me. This strangeness continued over several years. The colleague seemed almost always to disagree with anything I said and to criticize me at every opportunity. Our relationship was strained for many years. I finally got up the courage to ask the individual whether something was wrong. This was hard to do because I was unaware of any interaction that would have caused the colleague to behave in the way he or she did. The colleague at first hemmed and hawed a little, and then the truth came out. Many years ago, the colleague told me, I had written an article that the colleague interpreted as critical of his or her theory. I was flabbergasted. I could not even remember having written such an article.

I had my assistant do a search of my vita, and finally we were able to locate the article that apparently had offended my colleague. I did indeed mention the colleague's theory, but I thought I had done it in a basically favorable light. At the same time, I had expressed a disagreement with aspects of his theory, much as colleagues have expressed disagreement with mine. I spoke again to the colleague and explained that I certainly had not intended to derogate the colleague or the colleague's work. Eventually, we patched things up and even have become somewhat close. Holding a grudge is good for no one!

In one of my official roles I work with a colleague from another institution who seems to have no limit to the number of grudges he holds. He lashes out at people for the smallest reason, and seems to delight in petty revenge. He is a bitter malcontent, disliked by all the colleagues with whom he works. This is not a fate to aspire to. If you are one to hold grudges, you will find plenty of reasons to bear grudges, and plenty of people against whom to bear them. Heck, many, if not most of my colleagues who have reviewed my work at one time or another have not liked something I have written. Indeed, sometimes I have later not liked things I have written. The best advice: Get through whatever issues you have with someone, then move on. There is so much to life. Don't waste it being bitter.

▣ ▣ ▣ ▣ ▣ ▣ ▣

THINK FOR YOURSELF: *Why do people hold grudges? Are there any advantages to holding them? What are the disadvantages?*

PUT IT INTO PRACTICE: *Are you one to hold grudges? If so, what do they buy you? Is it time for you to move on, if only for your own good and peace of mind?*

Lesson 44
Stay Away From Exploiters and Parasites

In any field, there are people who will want to exploit you and there are people who, quite simply, are parasites. Exploiters look at relations with you totally in terms of what they can get out of the relationship. Usually, they are in positions of greater power than you are. Parasites include exploiters but also people who are in positions of equal or lesser power. What exploiters and parasites have in common is that they view relationships as wholly instrumental and one-directional—that is, in terms of what they can get out of you.

I have made a conscious decision to stay away from such people. The issue with them is not one of misunderstanding or of a lesson that both can learn: These people, in my experience, are dispositionally parasitic. And they do not change. The old maxim "Fool me once, shame on you; fool me twice, shame on me" applies in relationships with such people. Continuing to interact with them, unless you absolutely have to, means there is not only a problem with them but also a problem with you.

Sometimes, it is difficult to be rid of such people. For example, occasionally, such a person will be an academic adviser. In most programs, it is possible to change advisers. Other times, the person may be a department chair. Such a situation is extremely difficult, and one can only hope that the individual will not last in the position. Or one can think of moving. Usually, one can and should make the decision to stay away.

I'm not beyond falling into this trap. I once had a relationship with someone who was a parasite, but because I liked the person, I did not let go. Eventually, I realized I had no choice. The relationship was destructive to me and had no real value. I let go. I then wondered—what in the world took me so long?

THINK FOR YOURSELF: *Why do people stay in parasitic relationships, often even after they realize what the relationships are?*

PUT IT INTO PRACTICE: *Do you sometimes feel exploited, or do you exploit other people? If you feel exploited, can you extricate yourself from the relationship of exploitation? If you exploit others, can you transcend this aspect of your behavior to seek more mutually beneficial relationships? How will you do it?*

Lesson 45
Help Each Person Find His or Her Own Niche

I learned this lesson from Gordon Bower, my graduate adviser. Gordon has had many graduate students who distinguished themselves in their careers, perhaps more than anyone else that one can readily think of. One of the reasons is that, as I discuss briefly in Lesson 35, he allowed each graduate student to find his or her own niche. Although he was happy to have students work on his own line of investigation, he was equally happy to let them find their own distinct pursuit.

Students do their best and most creative work when they really love what they do. For this reason, I have encouraged my students to find something they really love. It may be related to something I already am doing, but then, it may not be. What works best for them, in the long run, works best for me.

It is important to realize that niche finding applies to jobs as well as research. Some years ago, one of my graduate students received two job offers, one from a very highly prestigious academic institution and the other from a less prestigious one. The second one was well known, but the first one was near the top of the academic pecking order. She asked me which job offer I thought she should take.

The answer might seem straightforward: Why not take the more prestigious offer? But it was not straightforward. The reason is that the kinds of interests she had seemed a better fit with the somewhat less prestigious place. In particular, she liked teaching quite a bit, and the second place seemed to emphasize teaching more than the first one.

Psychology 101½: The Unspoken Rules for Success in Academia, Second Edition, by R. J. Sternberg

I was young and foolish at the time—barely out of my 20s—and I gave her bad advice. I told her to take the more prestigious offer. She did, and it proved to be a mistake. She did not fit in. Several years later, she left, and eventually she ended up at a place that particularly values teaching.

The lesson learned, of course, is that students, like everyone, need to find a place where they fit. Fit is much more important than prestige. If one finds the right fit, one will do one's best work, and things will generally go as they should from there. In seeking a job, it is much more important to find out what the institution values than it is to find their rank order in some set of ratings. If your values match those of the institution, you are likely to be happy there. If you and they don't have the same values, you are unlikely to be happy, regardless of the institution's prestige.

As a mentor, friend, or colleague, do not use fear as your primary way of motivating people. Some people do what they do not because it is what they care about but because they are afraid of what will happen if they don't do it. They may be trying to fulfill their parents' wishes, or their significant other's, or their department chair's, or their mentor's, or whoever's. People rarely find their true niche when motivated primarily by fear. Nor do they do their best work. Whenever possible, encourage people to do something because they believe in it, not because they are afraid of what will happen to them if they don't.

You inevitably will encounter people who want your niche to be their niche: That is, they want you to fit into their life—their goals and expectations—but they don't much care about where you want to fit in. Avoid such people. Usually they are so self-centered that they don't even see it in themselves, as their world revolves exclusively around them. You want to get out of their world, because it has room for others only to the extent that the others are satellites who revolve around them.

THINK FOR YOURSELF: *What are the obstacles to people finding their own niches, and how can people overcome them?*

PUT IT INTO PRACTICE: *Do you try to help others achieve their own personal destinies, rather than the destiny you might want for them? If not, how can you let go enough so that you help others achieve what is good for them, not merely what you wish were good for them or even only what is good really just for you?*

Lesson 46
Give What You Hope to Get

The lesson "give what you hope to get" may sound like the Golden Rule. It is. I have found that, on average, you pretty much get in proportion to what you give in a career and that what goes around comes around. If you are nice to other people, in the long run, most of them probably will be nice to you. If you are nasty, in the long run, they probably won't be very nice to you either.

A problem with academia is that, superficially, at least, it sometimes seems more to value getting than giving. Just as successful business people may hog money, successful academics may hog cushy trips abroad, light teaching loads, or whatever. Human nature is probably no different as a function of the occupation people are in. But if you look at the most successful people in academia, among whom I count my own mentors, they are people who have given a great deal. Indeed, I doubt that, among the most successful people, one would find many who were selfish in their professional lives. They learned, one way or another, that you get back what you give.

I was once asked to meet with a team of visitors to my university. I was busy at the time and felt like the last thing I needed was yet another meeting. But it was important to the university and the group for me to have the meeting. I had it, expecting nothing in return. What I got in return was the establishment of a collaboration that has proved to be one of the better ones I've ever had. You give even a little, and you may be surprised by how much you get in return.

The advice to give what you hope to get may seem obvious even in a book of obvious advice. In my experience, however, not a lot of academics follow this Golden Rule. If I look back on my career, I would estimate that the ratio of people who have asked me for favors to those who have offered them runs about 20:1, at the very best. In other words, it is yet another piece of wisdom that people observe mostly in the breach. People know it. They don't do it. Maybe you can be, and will be, the welcome exception!

THINK FOR YOURSELF: *Why do some people expect to get a lot and give little? What do they say to themselves?*

PUT IT INTO PRACTICE: *Do you, in your life and career, give what you hope to get? If so, how? If not, why not and are you ready to change?*

Lesson 47
Understand the Benefits and Limits of Loyalty

One of the things I value most in my students and colleagues is loyalty. I have always rewarded it, and I still do. I think many other professionals in the field feel the same way. What do I mean by *loyalty*? It has a rather complex meaning, at least in an academic context. If people are loyal, it means that I can trust them implicitly. I can be confident that they say what they believe and mean it. They also are trustworthy in action. I know that when they represent us to others, they will do so in a fair and, I hope, reasonably positive light. They will work for my research group in the same way that we will work for them. They expect our relationship with them to be symmetrical . . . and they will never stab us in the back.

At the same time, I do not expect students or employees to lose opportunities to profit from others. Most of my primary advisees also work with other faculty members—and should. By working with several faculty members, they receive a variety of perspectives rather than just one.

Some people are reluctant to criticize friends or colleagues because they are afraid it will be perceived as disloyal. The opposite is true. If you are loyal to someone, you will tell that person his or her strengths, as well as weaknesses, and give the honest feedback loyalty merits.

Sometimes, unfortunately, the loyalty you bestow upon another is not reciprocated. You act toward the other in what you believe to be an honest

Psychology 101½: The Unspoken Rules for Success in Academia, Second Edition, by R. J. Sternberg
Copyright © 2017 by the American Psychological Association. All rights reserved.

and loyal way, and you are poorly repaid for it. In such cases, the answer is not to be disloyal toward the person, as he or she was toward you, but to eliminate or at least minimize to the extent possible your relationship. People who are double-crossers rarely do it just once. If someone is willing to admit to an error and pledges to do better next time, sure, give the person another chance. But if it happens again, you can expect it to keep happening, over and over.

I have a colleague who once was stabbed in the back by someone with whom she had worked very closely. The back-stab came as a total surprise. My colleague had been very loyal to the individual, and then, the individual spread a nasty lie about my colleague. What's sad is that the colleague had been warned by others of the man's treacherous nature but had not wanted to listen. Listen! Often, others see things that you just do not want to see. But when you listen, be critical and make your best effort to distinguish truth from mere gossip.

THINK FOR YOURSELF: *Why do people stab each other in the back, even sometimes when the people they stab in the back have been loyal to them?*

PUT IT INTO PRACTICE: *Are you loyal to those who merit your loyalty? Do you ever stab people in the back? If so, what can you expect in return?*

Lesson 48
Maintain Your Good Reputation

In academia, the most valuable thing you possess is not some computer or piece of lab equipment, but rather, your reputation. Careers are made or broken on the basis of reputations. You therefore should do all you can to protect your reputation. One thing you can do is to fulfill the commitments you make. If you become perceived as someone who "punks out," you will find fewer and fewer people asking you to do anything.

I remember being on a selection committee for an international conference, and the name of a distinguished scholar came up. Everyone would have liked to invite the scholar, and as it was a prestigious conference, perhaps the scholar also would have liked to be invited. We decided not to invite her, however, not because we did not think she would be a good speaker but because she had acquired a reputation for making and then not fulfilling commitments. And when she broke commitments, it usually was at the last minute, after it was too late to get someone else in her place. She had hurt her own reputation through not fulfilling commitments. Don't do the same with your reputation.

Nonfulfillment can take the form of breaking commitments or of meeting them in a mediocre way. If you agree to do something, give it your best. Otherwise, don't bother. You will acquire a good reputation if you give the jobs you undertake your best effort.

Psychology 101½: The Unspoken Rules for Success in Academia, Second Edition, by R. J. Sternberg
Copyright © 2017 by the American Psychological Association. All rights reserved.

There are many ways to harm your reputation—examples include harassing people, exploiting people, and acting in other unprofessional ways. Once you give up your reputation, you give up your most important asset in the field.

Sometimes, things come to pass in your life that harm your reputation but that are not your fault. You may be the victim of gossip, which is especially rife in the Internet age. Or someone may purposely seek to defame you. Or you find that people take legitimate disagreements you have with them as implying there is something basically wrong with you. Should you find yourself suffering unjustified reputational loss, you may wish to fight back. Two good primers on how to fight back are to be found in Sonnenfeld and Ward (2007) and in Ronson (2015). When you suffer unfair loss of reputation, silence is sometimes interpreted as acquiescence to the charges against you. The main issues you have to face are these: Is it worth your time and energy to fight back? What are the costs and benefits? For example, publicly fighting a charge against you sometimes just ends up publicizing the charge. Further, how likely are you to succeed? How could you fight effectively? Is the fight a matter of principle or a matter of pride? If it is a matter of principle, you should do it. If it is a matter of pride, please think twice!

THINK FOR YOURSELF: *What are the kinds of things people do that quickly destroy their reputations? Why do they do these things?*

PUT IT INTO PRACTICE: *What steps do you take to maintain your reputation? If and when you have suffered reputational loss, how have you handled it? How could you handle it better?*

Lesson 49

Acceptance Is Not Necessarily Good; Rejection, Not Necessarily Bad

After I had gotten a paper on linear-syllogistic reasoning accepted, I did a study on the development of linear-syllogistic reasoning. I was looking at what changed in children's information processing with age. I submitted the article to a journal.

After submitting the article, I found myself regretting that I had sent it to the journal. The more I thought about the study, the more trivial it seemed. All I had done was to take a paradigm I had used among adults and apply it with minor modifications to children of different ages. There seemed to be little original in such a study, and I began to worry that I would embarrass myself with the submission. I considered withdrawing it and then decided that instead I would let the study get rejected and die a natural death.

A few months later I got the reviews back on the article, and to my astonishment, I received three very positive reviews and was required to make only the most minor revisions to get the article published.

In contrast, I once submitted an article on an aspect of thinking to a second-string journal, figuring that it would not have a chance with a better journal. The article was rejected with rather scathing reviews that I felt were unfair. I decided to submit the article to a better journal, and to my surprise, the better journal accepted it with few revisions.

One would like to believe that good papers and grant proposals get accepted and bad ones get rejected. But although, on average, better articles or proposals are more likely to get accepted than bad ones, many factors affect the ultimate fate of a paper or proposal. I learned long ago to take editorial actions more or less with a grain of salt. The papers and proposals that are easiest to get accepted are often ones similar to my article on the development of linear-syllogistic reasoning: The article makes a modest contribution and, most important, offends no one. Often, more important pieces of work do offend someone, so they are more likely to be rejected. Indeed, I believe that the work that is most likely to be rejected is that which is very bad, in which case it is rejected because it is very bad, and that which is very good, in which case it is rejected because it threatens someone. Ultimately, you need to become your best judge and do what you do not because it pleases someone else but because it pleases you.

When I was a graduate student, Endel Tulving and I wrote a paper on the measurement of subjective organization in free recall. We worked hard on the paper and thought it was pretty good. We submitted it to the *Psychological Bulletin*. To my great consternation, it was rejected. It was only my second major submission to a journal, and I already felt like a failure.

Later, I was writing another paper on subjective organization, and I asked Tulving how I should cite the paper that we had had rejected. He told me to cite it as "Rejected by *Psychological Bulletin*." I couldn't believe what I was hearing. Here we had the embarrassment and ignominy of having an article rejected, and he wanted me to advertise it to the world!

At the time, I did not understand. Now I do. He thought it was a good paper, and I thought it was a good paper, and that was good enough for him. He was convinced that the paper was good, regardless of what the reviewers said, and he was willing to flaunt it. His pride was in his work, not in the journal that accepted or did not accept it.

P.S. It later was accepted by *Psychological Bulletin*.

THINK FOR YOURSELF: *What are the advantages of sometimes receiving rejections in life?*

PUT IT INTO PRACTICE: *Do you understand that what seems good in the short run sometimes turns out badly in the long run, and vice versa? Are you prepared, then, for what seem like good things at one time to go badly in the future, and for what seem like bad things at a given time to go well in the future?*

Lesson 50

Don't Accept Someone's Views Just Because He or She Is Supposed to Be an Authority

I have received a great deal of good advice from authorities in my career, but some of the worst advice I have received has also been from people in positions of authority. When I was interested in going to graduate school, I thought it would be a good idea to consult with my residential college dean regarding my future plans. (A residential college dean at Yale is in charge of providing career and other advice to several hundred undergraduate students.) I went to talk to the dean, and he welcomed me to his office. I told him I was thinking of going to graduate school. He told me that, basically, I was a technician and that because I was a technician, I should go to a school of education, since schools of education train technicians.

I was crushed by his advice. Here I had hoped to receive encouragement, and all I received was what seemed like cruel discouragement. Fortunately, I did not listen to the dean's advice and have had a more or less successful career in psychology. I learned that one should welcome advice but also evaluate it and take responsibility for making the ultimate decision.

I've had experiences like this throughout my life—the teacher who told me I had no foreign-language ability, the teachers who expected little of me because I did poorly on IQ tests as a child, the professor who recommended I not study psychology. Often, life is about not listening to authorities.

Perhaps that is why Todd Lubart and I titled our book on creativity *Defying the Crowd: Cultivating Creativity in a Culture of Conformity* (Sternberg & Lubart, 1995).

I have met so many people who have let offhand comments by persons in positions of authority destroy their possibilities. Don't be one of them. Make of yourself what you want to be.

THINK FOR YOURSELF: *Why are people so quick to accept positions taken by people in authority, even when a position is unreasonable or plain harmful?*

PUT IT INTO PRACTICE: *Do you show respect for authority but at the same time realizing that the voice of authority, like any other voice, is sometimes just wrong? Are you willing to have courage to stand up for your beliefs in the face of authorities if you are convinced of the rightness of your position?*

Lesson 51
Communicate Clearly

An attribute of successful people in many fields is that they tend to be good communicators. If you look at the most famous psychologists, most of them are not only gifted scholars or practitioners but good communicators as well. It therefore pays to develop your oral and written communication skills as much as you can. Some of the best-known psychologists of our time, such as Steven Pinker, have developed their reputations not only because they are good scientists but also because they are especially effective communicators. On the contrary, people who have poor communication skills may have wonderful ideas, but if they cannot convey them, the ideas will be lost to others.

There are exceptions. Jean Piaget's writing is very dense and hard to follow, but Piaget became one of the great psychological scholars of all time. However, Piaget's fame, at least in the United States, owes a great deal to effective communicators, such as John Flavell, who took up his cause and wrote books and articles explaining Piaget's work. Most of us will not have others to interpret for us. It therefore behooves us to learn to write and speak effectively.

Some years ago I attended a conference of psychologists, and two psychologists spoke in a symposium, back-to-back, on their work. One psychologist was a dynamic, effective communicator whose enthusiasm for her work was apparent to the entire world. The second psychologist was

Psychology 101½: The Unspoken Rules for Success in Academia, Second Edition, by R. J. Sternberg
Copyright © 2017 by the American Psychological Association. All rights reserved.

at least as good a researcher—arguably, better—but spoke in a dry mono-tone voice that threatened to put much of the audience to sleep. After the symposium, it was the effective communicator who had streams of people coming up to talk to her. The other psychologist, whose work was really quite interesting, attracted few people. The work may have been interest-ing, but she failed to communicate its interest; she sounded bored with her subject, so she bored everyone else as well.

If your communication skills are lacking, it will pay off royally for you to work on improving them. Books and courses are available on improving both oral and written communication (see, e.g., Pinker, 2014; Sternberg & Sternberg, in press). As an academic, you will spend much of your time communicating. Learn how to do it well. If you are just starting out, posters at conferences can be an excellent way to get some visibility. As you advance in the field, hopefully, you will be giving more and more invited talks!

People sometimes think that it is one's ideas that are important, not the way one states them. Forget it. Most people are not willing to sit in their chairs and decipher cryptic messages. If the message is not clear, an audience will assume it is because the ideas themselves are not clear.

Communication skills also include listening. Being an effective listener can be one of the greatest assets you have. People have so much to tell you, if only you are willing to hear and then listen to what they have to say. To the extent that this book has any good advice, it is largely because I have listened to the lessons that my mentors and colleagues have taught me.

THINK FOR YOURSELF: *How do communication skills matter in giving talks?*

PUT IT INTO PRACTICE: *Why are communication skills important to you personally? How can you work to improve your communication skills?*

Lesson 52
Be a Little Ahead of Others, but Not too Little or too Much

There are two kinds of contributions that I think psychologists need to be wary of: replications and advance forward incrementations. Now, let me explain what they are.

Exact replications involve trying to repeat exactly what researchers have done before. In *conceptual replications*, in contrast, the generality of a finding or kind of product is assessed by trying to replicate it under circumstances somewhat different from those that originally gave rise to it. Exact replications and conceptual replications help solidify the current state of a field (Sternberg, Kaufman, & Pretz, 2002). They definitely are not glamorous kinds of work. The goal is not to move a field forward so much as to establish that it really is where it is supposed to be. Thus, in science, if a finding is surprising, then a replication can help establish that the finding is a serious one. If the replication fails, then contributors in the field need to question whether they are where they have supposed themselves, or perhaps have hoped themselves, to be.

Conceptual replications are limiting cases in that they in some sense seem, at face value, to offer very little that is new in terms of the types of creative contributions that can be made. Yet such replications are important because they can help to establish either the validity or invalidity of contributions, or the utility or lack of utility of approaches, that have been offered. Without exact and conceptual replications, the field would

Psychology 101½: The Unspoken Rules for Success in Academia, Second Edition, by R. J. Sternberg

be (and probably often is) very susceptible to Type I errors (false alarms). In science, replications help ensure the solidity of the base of empirical findings upon which future researchers build. Lately, replications are in fashion in a way they never were before. The reason is that scientists have begun to question just how replicable publishable research is, in psychological science in particular, but also in science in general. The journal I edit, *Perspectives on Psychological Science*, has a section devoted to replications. But still, they do not represent glamorous work.

Researchers need to be careful of building careers on replications because they are considered perhaps the least creative type of contribution one can make. When one comes up for promotion or tenure, replications may not be as helpful as other kinds of research.

Advance forward incrementations occur when an idea is ahead of its time. The field is moving in a certain direction but is not yet ready to reach a given point ahead. Someone has an idea that leads to that point. The person pursues the idea and produces a work. Often the value of the work is not recognized at the time because the field cannot yet adequately understand the contribution of the new work. The creator accelerates beyond where others in his or her field are ready to go—often skipping a step that others will need to take. The value of the work may be recognized later than otherwise would be the case, or some other creator who has the idea at a more opportune time may end up getting credit for the idea.

For example, Alfred Binet is best known for his work on intelligence, but as pointed out by Siegler (1992), Binet also did work on the nature of expertise in outstanding chess play and on the validity of eyewitness testimony. The latter work, which did not fit even remotely into existing paradigms of the time, was largely ignored. By the second half of the 20th century, these and other topics that Binet had studied gained prominence. Binet, however, is virtually never cited in the current work on these topics.

In my own career, I once did a grant proposal on concept naturalness. When I got the reviews back, they were rather negative, saying that the idea of naturalness of concepts was itself unnatural. I believe I was too early, or perhaps not persuasive enough, because a few years later, concept naturalness research was all the rage. Being too much ahead of your time can result in your getting credit later than you thought you would.

But more often, it results in the person who had the idea at the right time getting credit.

So what should you do if you have an idea that is ahead of its time? The best thing you can do is to realize that presenting the idea to your proposed audience is not in itself enough; you also need to lead the audience to it. In other words, you have to take them down the conceptual path that will prepare them for the idea: In essence, you reduce the distance between where their heads are and where you want their heads to be. You provide greater guidance to them in helping them to understand the idea than you would have if the audience had been ready for the idea. In this way, you can help them to understand and appreciate an idea that otherwise might have sounded so foreign to them that they could not use it.

THINK FOR YOURSELF: *Should doing replications carry more prestige than it currently does?*

PUT IT INTO PRACTICE: *Are you willing to work hard to convince others of the value of your ideas? How do you convince other people of the value of your ideas, especially when at first others do not accept your ideas?*

Lesson 53
Let Others Do Your Bragging for You

John Flavell is one of the most distinguished cognitive–developmental psychologists of the generation ahead of me, and also one of the best liked. During his days as a professor at the University of Minnesota and at Stanford, he was well liked for many reasons, but certainly one of them is his deep-seated and genuine humility. Although he was an icon of his era, I never heard him brag about—or even recount—his own impressive string of successes. In general, I have found the very best people in the field to be surprisingly modest. The second string often is not.

I know another psychologist who cannot seem to stop bragging. Much of her bragging takes the form of name-dropping. She manages to get into almost any conversation all of the important people with whom she has interacted. Even in meetings, she somehow manages to brag about the connections she has established. Perhaps she thinks she is impressing others. Mostly what people say of her is that she is a name-dropper. She seems to be the only one who is impressed.

In general, I think psychologists fare better when they concentrate on doing their best work rather than on bragging about how good their work is. If you do good work, others will spread the word for you. If you do not, no amount of bragging on your part is likely to make much of a difference.

Another kind of bragging is overstating the importance of one's findings in a research paper. When scholars write papers, they often overstate their claims so that people will realize how important their findings are. But reviewers for journals usually make them tone down their claims. In this case, it is better to let the data speak for themselves rather than having to overspeak for the data.

□ □ □ □ □ □ □

THINK FOR YOURSELF: *Why is it less effective to brag than to let someone else give praise?*

PUT IT INTO PRACTICE: *Are there instances in which you toot your own horn when it would be better for someone else to toot it for you?*

Lesson 54

Look for Collaborators With Whom the Whole Is More Than the Sum of the Parts

I have worked in many different fields over the course of my career, and people sometimes ask me how I do it. One way is to have great collaborators. Over the years, I have been privileged to work with many wonderful collaborators—undergraduates, graduate students, postdoctoral students, and faculty members. Collaborators can be a key to your success. First, they will have ideas you will never think of. Second, they will stimulate you to have ideas you would not have had otherwise. Third, they will provide expertise you do not have. And fourth, they will make the job of doing research much more fun.

There are many projects that I never would have thought to have done without my collaborators. For example, in the early 2000s, I worked with collaborators who were interested in studies in a variety of cultures. So I let my collaborators lead me, in the same way that my own graduate adviser, Gordon Bower, often let his students lead him. The result was a series of articles on cultural studies of intelligence that were fun to work on and interesting to boot (e.g., Sternberg, 2012; Tan et al., 2009).

My collaborators and I have also done a number of international studies in exotic places, such as Jamaica, Kenya, Tanzania, Zambia, Taiwan, and India. These studies have yielded some of our most important findings. For example, in Kenya, we found negative correlations between tests of academic intelligence and practical intelligence, a very important result for our research program (Sternberg et al., 2001). But we never could have done any of these international studies without a team of people who wished to be involved in the research. Those who do not collaborate miss one of the great joys and opportunities of an academic career.

Here's the rub. You don't always get to choose your collaborators. Sometimes they are chosen for you, and sometimes they underperform. In these cases, your options are limited. One option is to have multiple group members shame underperformers into doing their share. A second option is to help the underperformers get their work done, even if it is not really your job. A third option is to see whether a higher authority can nudge the underperformer to get with the program. But in the end, in any collaboration, you are at the mercy of collaborators, for better but sometimes for worse.

THINK FOR YOURSELF: *How can one go about finding collaborators for whom the whole of one's research will be greater than the sum of its parts?*

PUT IT INTO PRACTICE: *How could increased collaboration further your agenda in research or in teaching? Are there new opportunities for collaboration that you might, in the future, seek out?*

Lesson 55

Be Respectful and Pleasant Toward Others as Much as Possible, but Don't Use Ingratiation

Being very pleasant with people, being civil toward them, and showing interest in them, their work, and their families typically does pay off. Many people do these things naturally. Others do not. In my experience, you should do these things if you can. The field of psychology, like many other fields, is founded in part on personal relationships. People with better interpersonal relationships will thus typically be at an advantage over those with poorer ones. I doubt that good personal relationships ever got me a grant or a journal acceptance. But I'm quite confident that they helped. And being rude is always a mistake, regardless of the circumstances. I have found that many people have long memories for rudeness, and it is not something for which you want to be remembered.

Some of the people at the very top of the field are not very good in personal relationships. If you make it to the top of the field, congratulations! You probably can afford to pay less attention to this advice than can some others. But very few people make it to the very top, and moreover, even those at the top still will be at an advantage if they treat others with respect and dignity.

In general, I have found that it always pays to treat people with respect, no matter who they are. I get e-mails from high school students that sometimes drive me up the wall. Many of them expect me to do their homework for them. But I try to answer them—very briefly but politely. It just does not pay to be disrespectful of people.

You will get reviews of articles that seem to have been written by morons. At times, you may review articles that appear to have been written by morons. Resist the temptation to tell the authors what you think of them! Never make ad hominem criticisms. Criticize the work, not the person. There is no need in academia for people to be uncivil toward each other. If you are uncivil, you do not show yourself to be clever but rude. People will think more highly of you if you keep the level of discourse professional and avoid personal attacks. And you will get better outcomes in all aspects of your career.

I once got a review of a paper I coauthored in which the reviewer said I should consider doing research in an area that is more consistent with the level of mental ability I bring to bear upon the task of research. I laughed when I saw the comment, although I must admit it stung. But I had seen similar savage reviews before, and I was not about to let the reviewer's personal hostility upset me. When directed against people earlier in their careers, such comments can be devastating, however. Really, no one has the right to make such comments, and it was, in my opinion, a mistake for the editor even to have circulated them.

Although you want to be respectful, you don't want to be ingratiating. Ingratiation is a delicate topic in academia. To what extent do you suck up to those in authority? Or should you do it at all?

When I was an assistant professor, I was in the office of a fellow assistant professor discussing something within. During the discussion, I happened to see the colleague's date book open, and in it, the names of virtually the entire senior faculty, who had been invited to dinner on different days. I thought to myself, "Oh no! I didn't know I was expected to invite all of the senior faculty to dinner. Now what?"

I never did invite the entire senior faculty to dinner. It just wasn't me. Later, I got tenure and the other faculty member did not. So the dinner invitations perhaps did not pay off as the colleague had hoped. My experience is that blatant flattery of someone in a position of authority typically is seen as such and does not produce very good results, except to label the individual engaging in it as a suck-up.

At the same time, it does pay to point out to people that you recognize their strengths and their contributions. That is not ingratiation. It is fair game. People often feel undervalued in academia. As I have said before, there seems to be much more negative feedback than positive feedback. So by all means, if you like what someone does, tell him or her. The individual will be glad to hear it, so long as it is sincere.

The greatest challenge I have faced, I think, was when, as an administrator, I had to raise money for my universities. Some donors want nothing more than sheer ingratiation. What I did instead was to try to find out something about their background and then commend them for their past achievements, which they invariably had. It made more sense to me than empty compliments. I hope they felt the same way!

THINK FOR YOURSELF: *How can one better show one's respect for others without being ingratiating?*

PUT IT INTO PRACTICE: *Do you have ways to impress people without having to suck up to them? Are you respectful of other scholars, even when you disagree with them or when you have questions about the quality of their work? How could you be more respectful?*

Lesson 56
Deal With the Impossible Problem of "Assassins"

We all hope it never happens, but we may acquire an "assassin" who is out to do us in. Sometimes, for whatever reason, someone wants to harm us emotionally, socially, or professionally, and that person just will not stop trying. It seems as though the person's mission in life is to bring us down.

It's happened to me. One person in the field has taken it upon himself or herself to discredit much of the work I have done. The individual is ideologically opposed to the kind of work I do on intelligence—for example, believing in innate racial differences whereas I do not, believing in the immutability of intelligence whereas I do not, believing in intelligence as a single entity whereas I do not, and so forth. But there are many scholars who disagree with me on a number of issues, and most of them do not write and publish personal attacks.

I wish I had wonderful advice for handling this problem in every situation, but I don't. Sometimes talking to the person helps; sometimes it does not. If you have a common superior, talking to the superior may help, but it may not, and in rare cases, it may hurt if word gets back to the assassin that you spoke to the superior. Fighting fire with fire (i.e., trying to hurt the assassin back) usually does not help either; it just gives you, as well as the assassin, a bad reputation. If you talk about what is being done to you, you risk spreading rumors that make you look bad. Ignoring the person may work and is, in my experience, usually the best way to handle such problems. I try as much as I can to stay away from assassins. Probably each case has to be handled individually. But you should be aware that such things do happen, regrettable though they may be. In the end, when I have replied to attacks by individuals, I have tried to limit my responses to the substance of the attack and completely ignore its personal aspects.

Why do people engage in such attacks, anyway? There are different reasons. Some are insecure and bolster themselves by taking others down. Some latch on parasitically, hoping to amass a reputation by attaching themselves to others who are better known than they are. Some probably believe that they are doing something virtuous by taking others down. And some are probably just aggressive people who look for outlets for their aggression, wherever they happen to find them. In the end, you want to stay away from these people because they thrive on conflict.

THINK FOR YOURSELF: *Is there any single best way to handle personal attacks, or does one have to modify one's strategy to suit the particular attack?*

PUT IT INTO PRACTICE: *Do you have techniques for handling people who viciously attack you? What do you do? What other strategies might you use?*

III
Institutions and Academia

Lesson 57
Find Your Mission and Define Success in Terms of Realizing It

Although I have studied intelligence for many years, it is only relatively recently that I have come to define intelligence not in terms of some arbitrary societal definition of success but rather in terms of personal definitions within a sociocultural context. In particular, I define *successful intelligence* (Sternberg, 2011) as the ability to achieve success, according to one's own definition of success, within one's sociocultural context. The message of this definition is that there is no one definition of success that works for everyone, either across societies or even within these societies. We all need to decide what success means for us. For some people, it might be as a musician; for others, as a plumber; for others, as a househusband; for others, as a mother; and for others, as a psychologist. If you are reading this book, there is a good chance that at least part of your definition of success is in terms of being a psychologist.

But it turns out that there is no one definition of success even for psychologists. Some psychologists succeed by being superb teachers, others by being superb researchers, others by being superb practitioners, and still others in other ways. And within each of these categories, there are many ways to succeed. We all need to find our own path. This need is why it is so important for mentors not to judge their mentees in terms of the extent to which the mentees reach the goals of the mentors but rather in terms of the extent to which the mentees reach their own goals.

If you look around you, there always will be people of your approximate age cohort who seem to be accomplishing more than you are. The question you need to ask is whether they are accomplishing more in terms of your personal goals or theirs. You need to focus on your goals for yourself, not other people's goals either for themselves or for you.

Over the course of my career, I have supervised many graduate students, postdoctoral students, and of course, undergraduate students as well. Some of my students have become academics; others have become management consultants, publishers' representatives, marketing consultants, statistical consultants, and so on. I view their success in terms of my own theory, which is to say, in terms of the extent to which they have furthered the accomplishment of their own goals. I would rather have a student become a successful management consultant than an unsuccessful academic (however the student may define success in his or her subsequent career).

Unfortunately, not every adviser is this supportive. If you decide to go nonacademic, you may have advisers or others try to convince you to pursue an academic career. Alternatively, if you decide to go academic, you may have people telling you to pursue a nonacademic career. In fact, over the course of your career, there will probably be many people who will try to set your goals for you. My advice is, well, to listen to their advice. But no one can set your goals for you. That is something you have to do. There will be all kinds of pressure to listen to and follow the advice of others. Resist the temptation to succumb. Do what you believe is right for you. There is no other way in which you can be and continue to become yourself. Only one person can set your mission: you!

Me? My professional mission in life has been to change the way people conceive of intelligence and related abilities. I have had only very limited success in this mission, but I'm still trying to fulfill it. The good thing is that, so far, I have succeeded much more in what ultimately has become my personal mission: to see my wife and five children find happiness and success in their lives.

▣ ▣ ▣ ▣ ▣ ▣ ▣

THINK FOR YOURSELF: *How does one go about finding
a mission in life?*

PUT IT INTO PRACTICE: *Have you defined just what your
mission is? Is your mission one that you can accomplish?
How would you know whether you accomplished
your mission?*

Lesson 58
The World Is Not Fair

In the course of my career, I have seen countless situations that seemed, to me at least, unfair. Some were only slightly unfair, such as someone winning an award who seemed not to have deserved it but who seemed to have the right connections whereas his or her competitors did not. Others were grossly unfair, such as the case of someone who was turned down for tenure at a major institution when someone else whose record was markedly inferior received tenure instead. There were people hired who should not have been, people not hired who should have been, grants funded that should not have been, and grants not funded that should have been. I sometimes have felt terribly unlucky in decisions and choices I have made. Luck has a way of distributing itself without regard to what people may think they merit.

You will find, over the course of a career, that luck averages out for many people, but not for all people. Chances are you will have some occasions when your luck is better than you expected, other occasions when your luck is worse. But it does not always average out. If you are in a fatal plane crash, as was my friend Joe Rigney, formerly a psychologist with the U.S. Navy, then your luck simply ran out for good. If you become ill when you are young, as did the noted paleontologist Stephen Gould, you are simply unlucky. Gould was able to fight off cancer early in his life, but then succumbed to it at the relatively early age of 60.

Unfairness can take many forms. It can take the form of bad luck in life, such as an early serious illness or death. It also can take the form, as it frequently does, of discrimination in the workplace on the basis of gender, ethnicity, religion, race, age, or other characteristics. Sometimes the discrimination is overt; more often, it is subtle. But it stings nevertheless and can interfere with one's career. One can and should combat it to some extent, but often it is pervasive, even moving with you when you move from one locale to another.

If you believe that life should be fair, you are at substantial risk, I believe, for becoming embittered. The reason is that even if a person's luck averages out, many of us find much more salient the bad luck than the good luck we have. So if we believe life should be fair, we are susceptible to thinking that it is unfair—to us. Don't waste your time. Anyone can find things about which to be bitter or cynical. I certainly can. You are much better off moving on and focusing on the positive things in your life. Research shows that people seem to have relatively stable average levels of happiness. That is, people tend to be happier or less happy people, almost without regard to what happens to them. You will have a happier life if you follow the oft-given advice that you are about as happy as you make up your mind to be.

One of the more notable examples I have seen is that of a colleague of mine. He and a collaborator invented an important construct in psychology. Someone else then popularized that construct. The individual who popularized the construct has probably received much more credit than the colleague who co-invented the construct. It's just not fair!

If the world of psychology, like the world beyond psychology, is so unfair, why even bother to make an effort to succeed? Well, there are several reasons. First, all systems have unfairness either built into them or as an incidental factor. So you can decide to do something else besides academic psychology, but you will soon discover unfairness in the new system you enter. Second, often things are unfair in the short run but tend to even out over the long run. So maybe you do not get one thing you want that you should have gotten, but then later you do get something you wanted that perhaps you should not have gotten. My experience is that over the long run things often (although not always) work out. Third, if everyone gave up when they discovered that the world of psychology can be unfair, no one would be left in it. So you need to learn how to survive in systems that are, to a greater or lesser extent, unfair, at least by our perception of them. The sooner you accept the fact that things are not necessarily fair, the sooner you can learn to cope with the way the world is, rather than the way many of us unrealistically wish the world were.

◨ ◨ ◨ ◨ ◨ ◨ ◨

THINK FOR YOURSELF: *How do people cope with the unfairness of the world? What ways of coping are more effective and what ways are less effective?*

PUT IT INTO PRACTICE: *Has the world sometimes treated you unfairly? If so, have you been able to get over it and move on? If you have not been, could you do so now, realizing that, even if you were treated unfairly, it will be better for your psychological health (and perhaps other people's as well) if you were able to move on?*

Lesson 59
The Ivory Tower Is Not Spotless

When I entered academia, I expected a life that never quite happened. I thought academics were interested primarily in ideas, put their personal feelings aside in debates, were generous in praise and kind in criticism, and on and on. No such luck. Most of the people I've dealt with are decent people. But some of them aren't. Some are arrogant. Some are selfish. Some are deceitful. And some are even destructive of others, for no obvious reason.

Dealing with such people is never easy. The best advice, really, is to avoid them if you can. That's always my first option. Sometimes the people are not so easily avoidable. If the person is your adviser, consider switching advisers. If the person is your department chair, consider whether there is any member of the university administration whom you can trust and speak to in confidence. But at the same time, realize that this strategy carries serious risks: The person you thought you could trust might, in fact, prove not to be trustworthy. If the untrustworthy person is a research collaborator, try to get through the current project and then never collaborate with him or her again.

It is not just people who can be disappointing; so can institutions. I have seen many people who were long loyal to their institutions and then discover that the loyalty went one way. One retired professor who spent

Psychology 101½: The Unspoken Rules for Success in Academia, Second Edition, by R. J. Sternberg

almost his entire career at a state university ended up suing the university, which seemed determined to rob him of the retirement he felt he deserved. Another person got into trouble with his university when an unjustified complaint was filed against him and the university seemingly sided with the complainant. I have learned that it pays to keep one's expectations for loyalty on the part of one's institution relatively modest.

Part of the problem is that it is not exactly the university that acts but rather the people behind it. The same is true of any organization. I once had an extremely rewarding relationship with a company for which I did consulting. I found myself becoming very loyal to the organization. Then the organization was bought by another one and the new management dropped me like a hot potato. The organization kept its old name, but the personnel were completely different. Institutions often get bad through bad management, but your relationship with the institution may or may not. Institutions are rarely better than the people in them, and when the people change, an institution that may at one time have been great can do downhill pretty fast. At the same time, institutions also can go uphill pretty fast.

One of the most painful experiences one has in academia—and in life in general—is betrayal. People whom you considered close colleagues may betray you; for example, something you disclosed in confidence might be disseminated as though you'd intended it as a story for the front page of the local newspaper. If you betray people, you will soon enough find yourself with no one to betray, because no one will trust you. If someone betrays you in a professional relationship, my advice is that you not wait for it to happen a second time. If you continue to trust that person, you are setting yourself up for further disasters.

I am surprised by the extent to which people sometimes dig their own graves (and I must admit that I have sometimes done it myself). The maxim I mentioned in Lesson 44 applies here, too: "Fool me once, shame on you; fool me twice, shame on me." Some people let themselves be fooled once, twice, thrice, and onward. They let one or more other people take advantage of them, and then do it again and again. Don't be one of those people. If someone mistreats you, do what you can to avoid being sucked into the same situation again.

▣ ▣ ▣ ▣ ▣ ▣ ▣

THINK FOR YOURSELF: *Why do people betray each other? Are betrayals inevitable in life?*

PUT IT INTO PRACTICE: *How do you handle disappointments of your expectations for people or institutions? What do you do well and what not so well? What could you do better?*

Lesson 60
Institutional Cultures
Are Slow to Change

I have worked in and visited various institutions over the years, sometimes repeatedly, and have been struck by how the most basic aspects
of organizational cultures are very slow to change (Sternberg, 2000).
If you are thinking of going to a place, and they tell you that it is in
a period of transition, watch out. A place that values mediocrity will
not change fast, if only because the people there will continue to hire
mediocre people who do not compete with them. A place that values
excellence probably will continue to value excellence because it will look
for the best people it can find. A place that is institutionally bureaucratic
will probably stay that way, because it often would take the bureaucracy
to reform itself, and most bureaucracies are slow to do so. Thus, if you
are promised change, be at least a little wary of what is likely to change
and what is not.

How modifiable an institution is has little to do with how good it is.
Some institutions are good but reluctant to change lest anything they do
make them worse. Some institutions are bad and are reluctant to change
because they are afraid to be anything but the way they are. Even when
institutions are not great at what they do, some people benefit from leaving things the way they are. It is crucial that you understand the culture
of an organization before you become a part of it. First of all, you are not
likely to change the culture. So if you are going to a place hoping to make

it better, be sure that the people in the place want to be better. If you go to a place where people do not want to change, you may become like them.

THINK FOR YOURSELF: *Why do institutions get stuck in old but nonoptimal ways of doing things?*

PUT IT INTO PRACTICE: *What kinds of actions can you take to try to make an institution a better place? More important, what kinds of actions are likely to work, and what kinds are not?*

Lesson 61
Fuse Teaching, Research, and Service

Opportunities to fuse together teaching, research, and service are surprisingly abundant. Consider some possible combinations.

Teaching and research naturally go together. I have gotten several of my ideas for research from teaching. For example, some of my research has been on teaching introductory psychology, and the ideas for this research flowed from my having taught the course. Some of the research I have published has emanated from joint projects with students that started as course projects. And some of the courses I have taught have emanated from my desire to do research in an area and to understand the area better by teaching about it and by discussing it with students.

Teaching and service also can go together naturally. Many teachers use service projects as opportunities for students to learn about psychology in action. For example, when I took a course in child psychology as a student, many students spent at least some time observing or even working in day care centers to learn about what they are like. Service projects can also feed back ideas to students and faculty alike. Students may write reports based on their service experience, and faculty may be able to talk about service experience in their lectures.

Finally, research and service can go together as well. Service can lead to research projects, for example, on understanding factors that contribute to successful day care or to adequate care in a homeless shelter. Research can also lead to service: Our studies of effects of parasitic infections on cognitive functioning of individuals in developing countries have led to treatment for such infections for many individuals who otherwise would never have been treated. University service also can be useful to you. You may meet new people, and as a result, become involved in joint teaching ventures, joint research ventures, or simply conversations that feed into your teaching or research. Although service is not the primary way to get teaching or research done, it can help.

THINK FOR YOURSELF: *Why is service even important in a career, given that it counts least in most institutions toward getting promotion or tenure?*

PUT IT INTO PRACTICE: *What are some ways in which you could better fuse teaching, research, and service? How might you implement them?*

Lesson 62
Know What's Expected of You

Many institutions value both teaching and research, but when the time comes for considering people for tenured positions, sometimes either teaching or research counts more than the other.

Sometimes the priorities of the institution will be made as clear as day to you. Other times they may not be quite so clear. You can find out what the priorities are in several ways. One is to ask the chair or the dean. It is always better to ask, say, the department chair, in writing, perhaps in an e-mail, and then to get back a written answer. A second way is to ask colleagues who are not in administrative positions, although their responses will have less authority. A third way is to observe who has gotten tenure and who has not. If everyone or no one has, then you probably need not worry. Your fate is out of your hands. But if the proportion is somewhere between 0 and 1, you should find out what it is that the people who did (or did not) get tenure had in common, if anything. And a final way is to look at who seems to be rewarded by the department in informal ways. Which people are favored, and why?

The distinctions, of course, get finer than ones of just preference for teaching or research. Some institutions value service a lot, some hardly at all. When it comes to research, some institutions value only certain kinds of research, say randomized-assignment controlled experiments; other institutions value a variety of research approaches. Similarly, with regard to teaching, some institutions give faculty members teaching credit for supervising individual students in research; others do not give such credit.

Another variable in the equation is something called *collegiality*. Roughly, it refers to how well you are viewed as contributing to the life of the department. Often, it really becomes how much people like you. Some departments will make perceived collegiality an explicit criterion for promotion or tenure. Others will let you figure it out for yourself. But most institutions do care about it, whatever they may say. What an institution values is often not stated explicitly anywhere. You need to find out for yourself.

⊡ ⊡ ⊡ ⊡ ⊡ ⊡ ⊡

THINK FOR YOURSELF: *How does one find out what an institution expects, given that many of the demands are not actually written down anywhere?*

PUT IT INTO PRACTICE: *What does your institution value in evaluating people at your level of advancement? Are your values a good match with those of your institution? If not, do you want to adapt (change yourself better to fit the values of the environment), shape (try to change the environment to be a better fit to you), or perhaps select another environment in which you will be a better fit?*

Lesson 63

Know the Rules and Regulations—
Both Formal and Informal—
That Affect You

I hate reading rulebooks and long lists of things I should and should not do. But, as noted above, these are times in which it really pays to know what is permissible and what is not. In the early 1970s, Stanley Milgram (see Milgram, 2009) carried out experiments in which he pretended that participants were unmercifully shocking an individual (who actually was a confederate of the experimenter). Although the participants were debriefed, they had to live with the knowledge that they had administered what they had thought were painful electric shocks (even though they were no such thing). Milgram was able to carry out what today would be viewed by many as an ethically challenged set of studies. Current rules would not allow such a study, at least not in the way it was done.

Times have changed for human subjects committees. When I started my career, most applications were approved with what today would seem like a perfunctory review. Today, reviews are very careful and detailed. Times also have changed for grants. When I started my career, it was fairly common for people to be loose about what they charged to grants and which activities they charged to which grants. Today, such looseness is no longer permissible. Many, perhaps most, of our grants and contracts are audited, and one has to be prepared to justify every expense. It is totally impermissible to fund under one grant activities that should be occurring under another grant, or to fund activities that are far removed from what you proposed in the grant proposal.

Professors have had to become much more careful in what they say to students, whether individually or in a group, so as to avoid charges—or even the whiff of—harassment of various kinds. Professors in the 1970s were not nearly so careful as they are today in what they said or did. It is not just a matter of harassment: Students today interact with professors differently from many years ago—for example, ways of addressing professors are often less formal. We all need to recognize that, as times change, we must change as well. In the course of a career, one has to change in many ways. One either changes or risks disaster.

THINK FOR YOURSELF: *How has society changed during the years you have been alive?*

PUT IT INTO PRACTICE: *Are there ways in which your behavior fails to recognize the norms of the present? If so, do you sometimes get into trouble for such behavior? And if so, how might you change, before it is too late?*

Lesson 64
Love It or Leave It

Most people go into academia because it is what they love. But some go into it because it is what they think they love. They then find out they were mistaken. What do you do if you find you have made a mistake, perhaps even a horrible mistake?

Obviously, we all have to decide the answer to this question for ourselves, but in my opinion, the best thing to do is get out if at all possible, the sooner the better. Sometimes graduate students drop out of our graduate program, and they may be perceived as "losers" by those who still are in the program. In my opinion, their dropping out shows the exact opposite. They have recognized that what they are doing is not the right thing for them, so they find something else to do. This is exactly the right attitude to have. If you are in the wrong business, find one that will make you happy. The extrinsic rewards of academia are not so great that it is worth staying in the career if you are unhappy with it. Find something else to do that better enables you to make the most of your strengths.

When I was a graduate student, one very successful fellow student stayed at Stanford for 1 year, and then dropped out to go to law school. He could have been a very successful psychologist, I think, but it wasn't for him. Today he is a famous constitutional lawyer. He did what he needed to do, as should we all.

I've been there myself. I've worked at five institutions of higher learning, meaning that I've left jobs at four of them. In only one case was it an easy decision. But we need to continually ask whether we are in the right place at the right time. Sometimes what works for someone at a given point in time ceases to work at another.

The older you get, the harder it is to admit either that you've made a mistake or that what you once loved to do, you no longer love any more. Yet, people who look back on their lives when they are older often regret it if they allowed themselves to get stuck. Therefore, periodically reassess whether you are still excited about what you are doing, and if you are not, consider other options.

THINK FOR YOURSELF: *How does one know when it is time to leave an institution?*

PUT IT INTO PRACTICE: *Are you excited about what you are doing in your work? If not, can you find a new direction for yourself, either in your present job or in some other job? Are you willing to at least give it a try?*

Lesson 65
Don't Assume That Good Ideas Sell Themselves:
SELL THEM

Everyone would like to assume that their wonderful, creative ideas will sell themselves. But as Galileo, Edvard Munch, Toni Morrison, Sylvia Plath, and millions of others have discovered, they do not. On the contrary, creative ideas are usually viewed with suspicion and distrust. Moreover, those who propose such ideas may be viewed with suspicion and distrust as well. Because people are comfortable with the ways in which they already think, and because they probably have a vested interest in their existing ways of thinking, it can be extremely difficult to dislodge them from these patterns.

One of the first colloquia I was invited to give was at a well-known testing company. I was very excited about the opportunity. I thought that this talk would be a great chance to show people at this company that they were on the wrong track in understanding intelligence. To my surprise, the talk did not go particularly well. In retrospect, I don't know why I'd thought it would. After all, this was an organization that had become extremely wealthy on the basis of conventional ideas about abilities. Why should they believe me? Moreover, what did I expect—that senior, established people in the field would hear me, curse themselves for having wasted their careers, and then become devotees of mine? Not realistic! I needed to sell them on my ideas, not expect they would buy into them

Psychology 101½: The Unspoken Rules for Success in Academia, Second Edition, by R. J. Sternberg

because they were good, or at least because I thought they were good. (The truth it that, in this instance, there was probably nothing I could have done successfully to sell my ideas to this crowd!) When you have creative ideas, remember that they generally will not sell themselves. You must sell them. And expect that the more creative the idea, the harder it will be to persuade others of its merit.

When I started as dean of arts and sciences at Tufts, I wanted to persuade various groups of stakeholders that we could do better in our undergraduate admissions processes. I pointed out that Tufts wanted to develop future leaders and that the admissions processes Tufts was using were not necessarily oriented toward selecting future leaders. It took me a year, but with help from collaborators, I was successful and the university did indeed change its admissions processes to better align with its mission of selecting and developing future leaders.

THINK FOR YOURSELF: *Why are people often so reluctant to accept new ideas?*

PUT IT INTO PRACTICE: *Do you understand that the more creative an idea is, the harder it is to persuade other people of its merit? Are you willing to work hard to persuade other people of the value of your creative ideas?*

Lesson 66
Invent Your Own "Game"

I have been told that the late Paul Torrance, a famous psychologist in the field of creativity, would advise his students to invent their own game. By that, he meant that creative individuals are not ones who follow the career paths of others, but rather, people who invent their own career path. I believe that this is very good advice.

My own career path has been traditional in some ways, untraditional in others. It is traditional in that I went to college, then graduate school, then to a job, interrupting my educational stream by only a semester to work in the Yale admissions office. But my career has been untraditional in other ways: for example, in the range of problems in psychology I have chosen to study (including, among other things, intelligence, creativity, wisdom, thinking styles, love, hate, and conflict resolution). My choice of research topics has never been governed by fads: I tend to study problems that relatively few other investigators study.

I sometimes have felt that I have paid a price for my unconventional career. I do not fit neatly into any one special interest group, so I always feel somewhat on the outside. Or it may just be my nature to feel as though I am on the outside. If I had to redo my career, however, I would not change that choice. I created my own game, have enjoyed the game, and have been willing to pay any price for inventing the game. And there have been many advantages too: There always will be some people who will respect you more, not less, if you go your own way. There may be a cost to inventing your own game, but you will always have a great benefit: You will have played the game you created, not one someone else created for you.

When I speak of inventing your own game, I wish to make it clear that I am referring to how you go about your work, not to how you relate to other people. You don't want to be a game player with other people—someone who takes advantage of others. When you take advantage of other people, you may think they do not notice. But the chances are that they do. And the chances are that, in the long run, they will want to have as little to do with you as possible. One of the characteristics I value most in people is that they are straightforward with me and forego being manipulative or taking advantage of others.

THINK FOR YOURSELF: *When others doubt your sincerity, how do you convince them that you have their best interests in mind?*

PUT IT INTO PRACTICE: *What is your path or purpose in your professional work? Is it your own path or one that someone invented for you? How can you make sure that whatever path you follow is one that is personally meaningful to, and satisfying for, you?*

Lesson 67

Nonthreatening Ideas Pay Off in the Short Run, but Threatening Ideas Often Pay Off in the Long Run

One issue you may have to deal with in the course of a career is that of work that threatens other people. For example, in my own career, one of the main topics I study is intelligence. I believe that unitary theories of intelligence (centered on a so-called general factor—g—of intelligence) are not fully adequate. Many people in the field particularly like unitary theories and believe me to be wrong. Some among them feel threatened by people who disagree with them, just as I am susceptible to feeling threatened by people who disagree with me. And sometimes people who feel threatened, for whatever reason, turn nasty.

My advice is to get used to it. No matter how polite you are, no matter how willing you are to see other sides, if you take a stand, you will find at least some people ready to be antagonized. Backing down does not always help. Some people go away when you back down; others, sensing weakness, attack even harder, figuring you will not have the guts to oppose them. I thus believe that you have to stand for what you believe in, and let the chips fall where they may.

Psychology 101½: The Unspoken Rules for Success in Academia, Second Edition, by R. J. Sternberg
Copyright © 2017 by the American Psychological Association. All rights reserved.

As president of the Federation of Associations in Behavioral and Brain Sciences, I had to deal with this kind of issue all the time. People in the various associations disagreed with me strongly on many issues. Some of them were very powerful in their associations, and a few were perhaps less scrupulous than I ideally would have hoped for. When I faced opposition from them, a loud voice in my head told me that I would lose. But I needed then, and need now, to stand up for what I believe in, and take the flak. That's what I believe I have been called on to do, and that's what I will do, uncomfortable though it may be.

THINK FOR YOURSELF: *What is an example of an idea that might be good but is nevertheless threatening to the educational system we have in this country?*

PUT IT INTO PRACTICE: *Are you willing to stand up for your beliefs even when those beliefs, and your standing up for them, antagonize some people? Do you have the courage to stand up for your beliefs even when the going gets rough? If not, would you consider changing yourself in this regard?*

Lesson 68
To Persuade Is as Important as to Inform

I sometimes say, only half-jokingly, that almost every business involves sales in some way. How does an academic career in psychology involve sales? Well, some of us spend much of our time giving talks, writing articles, and writing grant proposals to persuade people to see things the way we do. Whenever I give a talk, I realize that my audience has heard or will hear many people who disagree with what I have to say. It is my job, in part, to persuade them to see things in my way, at the same time that I recognize that, ultimately, the choice is theirs. The difference between the stereotype of the typical "used-car salesman" and me, I believe, is that the product I sell is my own and I truly believe in what I say. I know that no scientific theories represent a final word, but I believe my theories and work have something to offer, and I would like people to believe at least in aspects of them. So I recognize that whenever I write or speak, I am trying to persuade as well as to inform.

When you write an article for publication, obviously you want to inform readers of your ideas and where they came from. But other people will be writing articles with ideas that differ from yours. The challenge is not only to present your ideas but also to show why they are better than the competitive ideas others present.

I do not necessarily want people to believe everything I say. Ultimately, I expect they will combine ideas from many other people with their own ideas to come up with a synthesis that works for them.

▣ ▣ ▣ ▣ ▣ ▣ ▣

THINK FOR YOURSELF: *Why are scholars sometimes reluctant to view themselves as trying to "sell" ideas?*

PUT IT INTO PRACTICE: *How do you persuade people who disagree with you? What techniques have you found to work, and what techniques have not worked for you?*

IV
Problems and Tasks

Lesson 69
Never Get Stuck on Seeing a Problem in Just One Way

People sometimes get stuck on seeing a problem in one particular way. They start hitting their head against the wall, trying to figure out a solution to their problem as they define it. Don't get stuck. Always ask whether there is some way to redefine your problem. A good example of redefining a problem is summed up in the story of an executive at one of the biggest automobile companies in the Detroit area. The executive held a high-level position, and he loved his job and liked the money he made. However, he despised the person he worked for, and because of this, he decided to find a new job. He went to a headhunter, who assured him that a new job could be easily arranged. After this meeting, the executive went home and talked to his wife, who was teaching a unit on redefining problems as part of a course she was teaching on applied intelligence (Sternberg, 1986; Sternberg, Kaufman, & Grigorenko, 2008). The executive realized that he could apply what his wife was teaching to his own problem. He returned to the headhunter and gave the headhunter his boss's name. The headhunter found a new job for the executive's boss, which the boss—having no idea of what was going on—accepted. The executive then got his boss's job. The executive solved his problem by creatively redefining it.

In my own career, I was once stuck in a particularly irksome situation. I was very concerned about the fact that a certain colleague had what seemed to be a negative perception of my work. I started devoting more and more time to trying to make the colleague see the value of what I was doing. No change. Then I redefined the problem. I realized that it really did not matter a whole lot what this particular colleague thought. I would have liked to change his mind, but I could not. So I went on with my life. Once I redefined the problem, I was fine. The problem was not how to please the person, it was to put the person and his or her opinion of me aside and move on.

Most important, I believe, is not to get stuck seeing your life in one way. During my career, I have seen many people be profoundly disappointed that they did not get the job they hoped for, or did not get tenured, or did not get promoted, and so on. Others sought to find opportunity in their setback, seeing it as a chance to start a new phase of their life. As you might expect, those who saw the positive in their setback fared much better in their careers and in their lives than did those who were crushed by disappointment and even self-pity.

□ □ □ □ □ □ □

THINK FOR YOURSELF: *Why do people get stuck in their ways of seeing things? What's the problem?*

PUT IT INTO PRACTICE: *When you have a setback, do you bounce back? Do you look for opportunities in failures? Do you sometimes find that if things do not go your way, you just give up and refuse to keep trying to accomplish your goals?*

186

Lesson 70
Surmount Obstacles Flexibly

When I was very young, I became interested in intelligence and intelligence testing as a result of my own poor scores on intelligence tests. As a seventh grader, at the age of 13, I decided it would be interesting to do a science project on intelligence testing. I found the Stanford–Binet Intelligence Scales in the adult section of the local library and started giving the test to friends.

This decision proved not to be among the better decisions I have made in my life. The first person to whom I decided to give the test was a girl in whom I was romantically interested. At the time, I was somewhat shy and I thought—as a result of low social intelligence, no doubt—that giving the girl an intelligence test would help break the ice. I was wrong. A practical piece of advice, therefore, is that if you are ever romantically interested in someone, giving the person an IQ test is not a good way to begin a relationship with that person.

The next person to whom I decided to give the test was a fellow I had known from Cub Scouts. Unfortunately, that was not such a hot choice either. Unbeknown to me, my friend had a severe mental illness. Well, maybe it wasn't really a mental illness: He was a tattletale. My friend tattled to his mother, who reported me to the junior high school guidance counselor. Unfortunately, being a tattletale appeared to be contagious. The guidance counselor reported me to the head school psychologist. The head school psychologist spoke to me and threatened to burn the book that contained the test if I ever brought it into school again. He suggested I find another interest. Had I done so, I never would have done all the work I have done on intelligence, which has meant a great deal to my life, and I hope, something to the world. His opinion presented a major obstacle to me, especially as an early adolescent. However, because I surmounted that obstacle, I have been able to do research on intelligence, which has been very fulfilling for me.

Obstacles do not go away when one grows older. Indeed, to the extent one is creative and defies the crowd, obstacles are likely to increase. They can be of different kinds at different points in a career. For example, I have had periods when one article after another has gotten rejected: It has seemed as though my name on an article doomed the article to failure before I even wrote it. At other times, I have had strings of grant proposals rejected. I have wondered why I even bothered to write them when they all got turned down. Eventually, things balance out, and some articles start getting accepted and some grants start getting funded.

Some obstacles are immediate ones. One of the things I have discovered is that when one gives a talk, including an important one, such as a job talk, anything can go wrong. I have confronted PowerPoint setups that I was assured would work but that nevertheless did not work, microphones that were underpowered, rooms with layouts and furnishings that seemed to have been stolen from horror movies, switches from a Mac to a PC that did not work out, and worse. Sometimes I was told that the audience was knowledgeable and found out quickly that they were not; other times I was told that the audience knew little, and they were experts.

Probably the worst colloquium experience I've had was when I went to a university in the Boston area with my intelligence slides, arrived 20 minutes before the talk, and saw a poster advertising my talk on "The Nature of Love." (Well, maybe it was worse the time I was giving a talk, there was a fire alarm, everyone left, and almost no one came back afterward to hear the rest of the talk. In that case, they voted with their feet.) My host asked me whether I would like to use the 20 minutes to prepare, and I assured him I did. Basically, I had 20 minutes to generate a talk, and obviously audiovisual aids were out of the question.

The point is that, in the face of obstacles, the key is to be flexible. When I go to a talk, I try to have two methods of presentation ready. If PowerPoint fails, I have handouts as backups. Or if all projection fails, I can give my talk without any audiovisuals at all. I have a rough outline of the talks I give in my head, so that, in an emergency, I can give an approximation to that talk if I have to, even if I don't have the slides for it. It will not be a great approximation, but it will get me through.

Two job candidate interviews stick out in my mind. In one, the interviewee dropped her slides right before the talk. They became hopelessly out of order. She gave a great talk anyway. In the other case, a PowerPoint setup failed. The woman simply would not start her talk until the PowerPoint setup was fixed. The result was that she lost 20 minutes of her hour waiting for the setup to work. The first candidate got the job; the second did not. I ended up thinking, only half in jest, that search committees for psychology departments ought to arrange some kind of catastrophe for each speaker, and see how the speaker handles it. If she or he successfully negotiates the disaster, the department hires the person; if not, the department doesn't. After all, a career requires great flexibility; why not find out right from the start if the candidate has it?

I used to wonder, when I was younger, what it is that distinguishes people who succeed in their careers from people who did not. Is it some kind of ability? Some kind of luck? Or what? No doubt, ability and luck both matter. But I am convinced that sheer persistence in the face of obstacles is an awfully large factor in the equation. Over the years, I have seen many people who started off their careers successfully and then would encounter some kind of problem or other. Those who allowed themselves to be defeated would end up with their careers on hold, or worse, in tatters. They could not take the heat, so they got out of the kitchen. A career in psychology typically is fraught with difficult situations. It is easy to give up at any time. Many people believe that they are the only ones encountering problems—experiencing the loss of a parent, a divorce, a health problem, a string of rejections, or whatever. But the truth is that, at some time or other, many people experience such losses. The question is not whether one will encounter obstacles. One will. The question is what one will do in the face of obstacles. Few attributes are more important than the willingness flexibly to surmount obstacles, no matter how insurmountable they may seem at the time.

If there is one point this lesson should make clear, it is that, as often as not, the main obstacles to your success are within you. There are any number of ways you can become the greatest obstacle to your own success. You can engage in self-defeating ruminations. You can sabotage yourself by doing work you know is not your best. You can decide that things will not go well, and thereby set them up to not go well.

Seligman (2006) argued that one of the best predictors of success in life is an optimistic stance. People who are optimistic often create the circumstances whereby their optimism ultimately will be justified; people who are pessimistic often create circumstances that result in defeat. So if you want to reach your goals and defy the obstacles to achieving them, maintain an optimistic stance. It will not guarantee you success. But it will go a long way.

At the same time, there will sometimes be obstacles that you make every effort to surmount, and you just cannot do so. Sometimes there are things we really want in life, and for whatever reason, they are just not attainable, no matter how hard we strive. It is for this reason that, in life, it is important always to have a Plan B, just in case your Plan A fails.

THINK FOR YOURSELF: *What kinds of obstacles in life are hardest to confront? Why are they the hardest?*

PUT IT INTO PRACTICE: *What kinds of obstacles have you faced in your life? Have you viewed obstacles as temporary challenges or permanent roadblocks? How can you engineer better responses to the obstacles you confront?*

Lesson 71
Nip Problems in the Bud

Inevitably, there will be times in your career when a problem is looming and you will be tempted to do nothing about it—to let it go. A lesson I have learned during my career is that often, if you do nothing early on, what starts off as a small problem becomes a big problem later on. It is better to deal with the problem, if you can, before it becomes a large one.

I have seen the problem in many different forms. One is personnel. I directed a center where teamwork and positive mutual support were our watchwords. We tried very hard to hire people who would be positive and mutually supportive toward each other. But inevitably, it seems, we made mistakes.

Sometimes someone joins my lab group who is not a team player and, often, is not a constructive influence either. What's to be done? I try to point out to the individual, in a constructive way, what is not going well. If repeated attempts to encourage the individual to change his or her behavior fail, I counsel the individual to look elsewhere for employment. Or she or he may decide to look elsewhere without such counsel. After all, my lab is not the perfect environment for everyone, and there is no shame in finding that the fit just is not there. Whoever makes the decision, I have found that such rapid attention to and remediation of problems is the way to go. Problems only very rarely solve themselves; more often, they get worse over time if nothing is done.

If you have conflicts with an adviser, it often is hard to talk about them with the adviser. But in my experience, leaving conflicts to simmer almost inevitably results in their getting worse and escalating over time. It is almost always better to try to talk things out civilly and respectfully. If the conversations do not go well, you may need mediation, such as from a departmental administrator.

One can see the same thing happen to graduate students and assistant professors who are just starting out as junior faculty. You do them no favor by overlooking things and hoping they will learn if you say nothing. In fact, I have found that most people welcome counseling but may be too shy to request it. Most people want to succeed and are grateful when you help them do so.

The same thing that applies to others applies to oneself as well. Sometimes I have seen signs that my relations with a particular individual are going "south." For whatever reason, one interaction does not go so well, then another doesn't, and then another. Soon there is a noticeable chill in our interpersonal relationship. Wherever possible, I have tried to speak with the person as soon as I see things going on the wrong track. Although an attempt to clear the air does not always work, it is surprising, in my experience, how often it does.

I once made a serious mistake in taking a job. I was not a good fit with the job, the people who surrounded me, or the values of the institution. Initially, I had thought I was, but it quickly became clear I was wrong. Having seen students of mine make a mistake in accepting a posting, I was surprised to find myself in the same position they had been in. But they had been younger when they made their mistake, and I was older and thought that, by my age, I should have known better. It's much easier to admit to a mistake when you're younger than when you're older. Nevertheless, I resigned and left the job after a very brief stint. I can't say I nipped the problem in the bud entirely, but neither did I let it fester for year after year.

▣ ▣ ▣ ▣ ▣ ▣ ▣

THINK FOR YOURSELF: *What techniques can you use to ensure that, when a problem arises, you will handle it quickly and expeditiously?*

PUT IT INTO PRACTICE: *Do you ever start to rationalize when things go wrong, hoping somehow to stall for time? When you rationalize, do you actually convince yourself or do you retain your doubts? How could you better convince yourself to move on than to remain with your mistaken decision?*

Lesson 72
Pick Important Problems on Which to Work

Like many other psychologists, I have spent long days attending conventions and other meetings where I would sit in on presentations and symposia whose only conceivable interest seemed to be that the presentation of the paper by the author may have paved the way for him or her to get funding to attend the conference. But, of course, excruciatingly boring material is not limited to conferences (or, occasionally, books of advice!). If you open the pages of a typical journal, you may find the typical issue contains only a few articles of interest to you, with at least some of the other articles defying any guess as to who would have wanted to spend the time to study whatever the authors were studying.

Why do some people devote so many resources to problems of so little interest to anyone but themselves and perhaps a handful of others? And how can they be satisfied writing articles that few people will read and giving talks that few people will want to listen to? One possibility is that there is a problem in our system of graduate education. I think that we place so much emphasis on how to solve problems that, at times, we forget about the importance of selecting good problems in the first place. The result is that the work that is done is often very fine and careful work on problems of little interest.

Another possibility for why an individual might pursue a problem that is interesting to him or her but to few others is that he or she may see merit in a problem that others simply do not yet see. We need always to remember that our judgments are, at bottom, nothing more than judgments. Some of the best work in the field has been that which opens up new problem areas that had been neglected earlier. So there is always the possibility that a problem that seems uninteresting at one point will seem interesting at another. For example, the problem of the nature of consciousness has gone in and out of fashion in psychology, at times seeming central, at other times seeming peripheral, and at still other times (as in the heyday of behaviorism) not seeming to be a real problem at all.

How can you tell if a problem is interesting, scientifically or otherwise? There is no guaranteed way of knowing, but you can certainly take steps to gauge interest. First, try to state—preferably in writing—why anyone in his or her right mind should be interested in the problem. If you cannot think of reasons, that may be a bad sign. Most speakers and many article writers seem to leave it to their audience to figure out why the problem is important. Don't! Figure it out and state it for yourself. A second thing you can do is to try briefly describing the problem and why you think it is important to psychologists who do not specialize in your field. Ask them frankly if they think the problem is interesting, and why or why not? A third thing you can do is to explain it to a layperson who has no training whatsoever in psychology. Does this individual find the work interesting?

Some psychologists would say that it does not matter what laypeople think. I think it does. First, laypeople often have the best sense of what problems are boring, because they have no vested interest in what psychologists do. Second, laypeople (e.g., Congresspeople) are the ones who decide what money is to be allocated for research funding. Third, when you teach psychology to undergraduate students, you are teaching to laypeople. If the research they learn about is boring, why will they want to pursue psychology as a field beyond the first course they take in it?

Zuckerman (1983) found that the most distinguished scientists were distinguished by virtue of their taste in problems. I thus emphasize with my own students that the most important issue they can confront is not how to solve a problem but whether the problem is even worth solving in the first place.

In choosing problems, some laypersons, and even some psychologists, have the tendency to believe that the more complex something is, the more impressive it is. I have found in my career, however, that the simplest ideas often are the ones that have the most power.

For example, two of the greatest psychologists of the generation of psychologists before me would certainly be Amos Tversky and Daniel Kahneman. They achieved their greatest fame, perhaps, for their work on heuristics and biases. For example, they showed how often people will use what they called the *availability heuristic* (Kahneman, 2013; Tversky & Kahneman, 1973), which is simply the recalling to mind of information one has heard recently or often. The idea is simple, the experiments they used to demonstrate the heuristic were simple, and yet the idea proved to have extraordinary power in explaining, at some level, many puzzling phenomena in the judgment and decision-making literature, as well as many puzzles in everyday life, such as why people are more afraid of plane crashes than of car crashes, even though many more people die in car than in plane crashes. According to Tversky and Kahneman (1973), people are more afraid of the latter because information about plane crashes is far more prominent in the media, and therefore much more easily retrievable, than information about car crashes.

The point is that often the simplest ideas are the most powerful. I have often felt that if I cannot explain what I am working on in a couple of sentences, then something is wrong.

Of course, I could also explain it in a book. But the core idea should be easily explicable. That is the elegance of Tversky and Kahneman's work. So when choosing a problem, go for the important one. You may find that it is important not because it is so complex, but rather, because it is so simple.

THINK FOR YOURSELF: *What makes a scientific problem important? What makes any problem important?*

PUT IT INTO PRACTICE: *Do you consider whether the scientific problems on which you work are worthy of your effort? If so, how do you decide whether a scientific problem is worth your time or effort? What do you do if you conclude that it isn't?*

Lesson 73
Be Guided by Problems, Not Methods or Fields

It is said that carpenters will always find things on which to use a hammer. The metaphor suggests that we all have sets of tools and then look for problems that can be solved using these tools. The downside of this approach is that we tend to ignore or shun anything that does not lend itself to, well, hammering, or whatever kind of work we do. So we may pass up countless opportunities just because our hammer does not lend itself to these opportunities. People become fixated on methods, or on fields, rather than on problems.

Field fixation can be as damaging to the understanding of psychological phenomena as is methodological fixation (Sternberg & Grigorenko, 2007). Psychology is divided into areas such as biological psychology, clinical psychology, cognitive psychology, developmental psychology, industrial/organizational psychology, social psychology, personality psychology, and so forth. Departments often organize the specializations of their professors in this way; graduate programs are usually structured in this way, and jobs are typically advertised in this way. This organization of the field, departments, graduate programs, and jobs is less than optimal. It encourages division rather than unification.

Several factors play a role in maintaining the current suboptimal organization of psychology, as I outline here.

- *Tradition.* First, and foremost, it is the way things have been done for a long time. When a system of organization is entrenched, people tend to accept it as a given. For example, most psychology departments have chairpersons, but members of those departments probably do not spend a lot of time questioning whether they should have chairpersons—they just accept this system of organization. Of course, new fields within psychology come and go. For example, evolutionary psychology and health psychology are relative newcomers to the roster of fields of psychology. They have already become an integral part of the field of psychological science as a whole. Other fields, such as ethology, no longer are very integral to psychological science and have been largely subsumed by other specializations.

- *Vested interest.* Second, once a discipline, such as psychology, has been organized in a certain way, people in the discipline acquire a vested interest in maintaining that organization, much as people gain a vested interest in maintaining any system that seemingly has worked for them in the past. For example, most cognitive psychologists were trained as cognitive psychologists, and personality psychologists as personality psychologists. Were the field suddenly to reorganize, current scholars and practitioners might quickly find themselves without the kind of knowledge base and even socially organized field of inquiry that would allow them to continue to function successfully.

- *The need to specialize.* Third, no one can specialize in everything. Students of psychology need to specialize in some way, and structuring psychology in terms of fields has been viewed as a sensible way to define specializations. Thus, someone who specializes in social psychology will be expected to know about a series of related phenomena, such as impression formation, attribution, and stereotyping. Or someone who specializes in cognitive psychology will be expected to know about a set of related phenomena, such as perception, memory, and thinking. And successively greater levels of specialization ultimately may be encouraged, such as in cognitive approaches to memory, to implicit memory, or to the use of priming methodology in studying implicit memory.

I believe that the current organization of the field is distinctly suboptimal and even maladaptive, for the following reasons (Sternberg, 2006; Sternberg & Grigorenko, 2007).

- *The field could be organized better to understand psychological phenomena.* Examples of psychological phenomena include memory,

199

intelligence, dyslexia, attachment, creativity, prejudice, and amnesia. None of these phenomena are best studied within a specialized field of psychology.

For example, although memory can be investigated as a cognitive phenomenon, it can, and should, be studied through the techniques of several other fields: biological psychology and cognitive neuroscience (e.g., in attempts to find out where in the brain memories are stored), clinical psychology (e.g., in the conflict over repressed memories), social psychology (e.g., in preferential memory for self-referential memories), and behavioral genetics (e.g., in the heritability of memory characteristics), to name just some of the relevant fields. Someone studying memory only through one approach or set of techniques will understand only part of the phenomenon.

Similarly, extraversion can be, and has been, studied from personality, differential, biological, cognitive, social, cultural, and other points of view. Someone studying extraversion from only one of these points of view—let's say, personality—almost certainly will understand the phenomenon only in a narrow way, in terms of, say, extraversion as a trait, without fully appreciating the role of biological or cognitive processes, or of culture, for that matter.

The same argument can be applied to virtually any psychological phenomenon. By subsuming psychological phenomena under fields of psychology, the discipline encourages a narrow view rather than a broad approach to understanding psychological phenomena. But you will do better work if you take a broad approach to phenomena and educate yourself broadly so that you are able to take such an approach.

- *Organizing by fields can isolate individuals who study the same phenomena.* Two individuals within a psychology department may both study attachment, for example, but if one is in personality psychology and another in developmental psychology, they may have little interaction. This is because in a typical department, students and professors are located next to—and attend the same meetings and read the same journals as—others in their field regardless of the phenomena being studied.
- *The current organization may create false oppositions between individuals or groups studying phenomena from different vantage points.* Here's an example: Individuals studying memory from a cognitive perspective may never quite understand the work of those studying memory from a clinical standpoint; this can lead

to a sense of hostility toward the viewpoints of those who do not understand their "preferred" way of studying memory. Or individuals studying love from social psychological versus clinical points of view may (and sometimes do) see themselves in opposition, as though there were a uniquely correct approach to studying a psychological phenomenon.

- *The current system tends to marginalize psychological phenomena that fall outside the boundaries of a specific field.* For example, psychological phenomena, such as imagination, motivation, or emotion, may tend to be ignored in a department if they are not seen as part of the core of a field. This also extends to the people studying such phenomena. They may have difficulty getting hired because hiring is often done by area, and the people studying phenomena at the interface of fields of psychology may be perceived as not fitting neatly into any one area. In turn, faculty in a given area may not want to hire such people if they feel that they will not get the full benefit of a slot or that such individuals will not contribute adequately to graduate (or even undergraduate) training in that so-called core field.

- *Research may tilt toward issues to which a limited set of tools may be applied.* The current system essentially equips students with a set of tools (e.g., the methods of developmental psychology, or cognitive neuroscience, or social psychology, or mathematical psychology). Instead of being driven by substantive issues, the system then encourages students to go in search of a phenomenon for which they can use their tools, much in the way a carpenter might seek to find objects on which he or she can use a hammer.

- *The current system can discourage new ways of studying problems.* If someone wishes to educate students in terms of the existing boundaries of fields, they will encounter little problem. But if they want to cross those boundaries, other faculty may worry that the individual will not be properly trained in a field, or may have trouble getting a job, or may not fit into the departmental structure. And in truth, they may be justified in all these concerns.

- *Perhaps most important, the traditional disciplinary approach of largely subsuming psychological phenomena under fields of study, rather than the other way around, leads psychologists to confuse aspects of phenomena with the phenomena as a whole.* This confusion is analogous to the use of synecdoche in speech, in which one substitutes a part for a whole (e.g., *crown* for "kingdom"), except that unlike poets or other writers, psychologists are unaware of

201

their use of this device. The psychologists believe they are studying the whole phenomenon when in fact they are studying only a small part of it.

Consider the well-worn parable of the blind men each touching a different part of the elephant and each being convinced that he is touching a different animal. In psychology, the situation is like always touching the same part of a phenomenon and thinking that this part tells you all you need to know to understand the whole phenomenon. Here are two examples.

In the study of human intelligence, psychometricians may keep discovering a "general factor" and thus become convinced that the general factor largely "explains" intelligence. Biological psychologists may find a spot or two in the brain that lights up during the fMRI or PET-scan analysis of the commission of cognitive tasks and become convinced that these parts of the brain fully explain intelligence. Cultural psychologists may find wide cultural differences in notions of the nature of intelligence, and become convinced that intelligence is best explained simply as a cultural invention. Each psychologist touches a different part of the metaphorical elephant, and becomes convinced that part represents the whole (and fairly simple) animal.

In general, scientists who are not well trained in one another's techniques are likely to be suspicious of the other's techniques and of the conclusions drawn from them. Instead, these scientists probably will continue to do research within their own paradigm, which keeps supporting their views and thereby reinforces their confidence that they are right and that those who adhere to a paradigm from some other field are misguided.

A more sensible and psychologically justifiable way of organizing psychology as a discipline, and in departments and graduate study in psychology, is in terms of psychological phenomena. We have advocated this different way of organizing the discipline of psychology because psychological phenomena are not arbitrary, but the so-called fields of psychology largely are (Sternberg, 2006; Sternberg & Grigorenko, 2007).

Under this approach, an individual might choose to specialize in a set of related phenomena, such as learning and memory, or stereotyping and prejudice, or motivation and emotion, and then study the phenomenon or phenomena of interest from multiple points of view. The individual thus would reach a fuller understanding of the phenomenon being studied because he or she would not be limited by a set of assumptions or methods drawn from only one field of psychology.

The proposal here carries with it several advantages that are largely complementary to the disadvantages of the present field-based approach that currently dominates the discipline. People might very well end up specializing in several related psychological phenomena, but they would understand these phenomena broadly rather than narrowly, which is certainly an advantage if one's goal is comprehensive psychological understanding. Psychology would be less susceptible to tendencies that field-based organization encourages: narrowness, isolation, false oppositions, marginalization, largely method-driven rather than phenomenon-driven approaches to research, discouragement of new ways of approaching psychological phenomena, and confusion of the part with the whole.

THINK FOR YOURSELF: *What leads a field in psychology to succeed over the long term, or else to be replaced or subsumed by other fields?*

PUT IT INTO PRACTICE: *What drives your research? Are there phenomena that are personally meaningful to you, aside from current fads or trends in the field? If not, can you find problems that are personally meaningful and hence will be highly motivating for you to study?*

Lesson 74
When You Can't Start but Have to, Start Small

One of the unhappier but also more common experiences in academic research is getting stuck—whether it be in starting to write or revise a paper or a book, in preparing a lecture, or in anything else. It took me forever to start writing my dissertation. The task just seemed too large. But then I started writing the method section. I knew I could do that because all I did was literally recount what I had done. And it all flowed from there.

Some years ago, I signed a contract to write an introductory psychology textbook. I set a deadline for starting on the text. It came and went, and nothing happened. So I set myself another deadline. That deadline also passed without even a word's making its way onto paper. I then set a third deadline and decided that this time I meant it. But as the deadline approached, the task seemed so daunting that I felt paralyzed and could not see my way through to starting the writing of the book.

I then realized that I had to redefine the problem. I had planned to start the book from the beginning, beginning with Chapter 1, which was to be on the nature of psychology. But the first chapter of an introductory psychology text is often one of the most difficult to write. I was setting myself up for failure. Then I decided to change strategy. I asked myself which chapter would be absolutely the easiest one to write, and I settled on the chapter on intelligence because that is my main area of expertise. So I started writing the chapter on intelligence, and that was a task I could

Psychology 101½: The Unspoken Rules for Success in Academia, Second Edition, by R. J. Sternberg

handle. Then, after that chapter was done, I took on the second-easiest chapter, on thinking, another area about which I felt well-informed. Again, I was able to complete the chapter without too much difficulty. By now I was well underway and no longer had to do the chapters in order of ease. But by starting with the easiest task, I made it possible for me to get started and then to have the motivation to keep going.

THINK FOR YOURSELF: *Why does starting small often help you accomplish your goals in a way that "starting big" does not?*

PUT IT INTO PRACTICE: *Do you have any large tasks on which you are currently procrastinating? How could you divide them into smaller subtasks so that the whole project no longer seems so daunting?*

Lesson 75
Most Things Take Longer Than You Think They Will

It is common in a career to discover that things take longer, and often quite a bit longer, than you expect them to. For this reason, it is important to begin projects, especially those with a short deadline, in a timely fashion. Otherwise, you risk missing deadlines. Endel Tulving once told me this, and he proved to be dead-on accurate.

I first discovered this lesson in its full force in my first year of teaching. I was teaching four semester courses that year—two each semester—plus attempting to do administrative chores for the department and also do new research and write up my dissertation as a book. Also, I had this idea that I could teach a course on intelligence and use the lectures to write a book on theories of intelligence.

So each day, I set aside some time to prepare the lectures in a format that could later serve as a book. But as the semester wore on, I got further and further behind on the book. I could barely keep up with the lectures. Eventually, I realized that I just could not keep up with the lectures in a format that would make them a book. That was in 1975. I did eventually write the book. It was published 15 years later, in 1990! I no longer try to simultaneously teach a course and create books from the lectures I give. Things take longer than one thinks.

This revision of *Psychology 101½* is a perfect example of a task that has taken longer than I expected it would. I initially gave it a month; then it was two; then it was three; finally it was four. It's really hard to find tasks that get done more quickly than one ever expected!

Think for Yourself: *Why do things often take longer than you expect?*

Put It Into Practice: *Do you start on assignments early, realizing that they will take longer than you expect? Do you keep track of your progress on tasks to make sure you stay on time? How could you better monitor your progress toward completion of important tasks?*

Lesson 76
Seek the Action in the Interactions

Psychologists waste an inordinate amount of time seeking to answer questions such as, "Is heredity or environment responsible for one's intelligence?" or more generally, "Is X or Y responsible for phenomenon Z?" But such dilemmas often are false dichotomies because different factors frequently interact with each other. For example, heredity and environment interact in the development of intelligence or almost anything else. A person with great genes who has been brought up in a closet most likely will not develop into a brilliant scientist. Correspondingly, one has to have "healthy" genes to be able to benefit from an enriched environment. Someone born with a severe and incurable genetic disorder may not benefit from any environment, no matter how favorable it is.

There are countless examples of false dichotomies. In the 1970s, when I was in graduate school, a big question was whether human information processing is serial or parallel. Another was whether human thought relies on images or propositions. These kinds of simplistic *either/or*s rarely help elucidate much about human thinking. Most psychological processes can be one thing or another, depending on the circumstances under which they are executed. Psychologists thus need to understand how structures and processes interact with the environment to produce the phenomena we observe in the world.

Anything can be carried too far. Interactions are so complex that one can get lost in them. Few studies have the power to reliably spot interactions beyond the third order. Science probably will never grasp all the complexities of human behavior. But it can go quite far with the techniques available to it. Thus, you want to recognize complexity but not allow yourself to become overwhelmed by it. Science is about reducing complex phenomena. It does not necessarily understand the full complexity of natural or other phenomena.

Keep in mind also that very few psychological phenomena are singly determined—meaning that they have just one cause and one cause only—and probably very few admit to no interactions. If we look at intelligence, personality, emotion, or motivation, each of them is complexly determined. Trying to find "the cause" of anything is likely to be a wild goose chase. Most things are multiply determined.

THINK FOR YOURSELF: *What is an example of a false dichotomy of which you are aware?*

PUT IT INTO PRACTICE: *What kinds of interactions are affecting your career right now? Are there things you can do to improve them?*

Lesson 77

Seek Syntheses of Ideas That on the Surface Seem Incompatible

People have different styles of work. One style that has worked well, at least for me, is to synthesize ideas that in the past have seemed incompatible. For example, early in my career I was busy at work trying to synthesize what sometimes had been seen as two very different traditions in psychology, the cognitive–experimental tradition and the psychometric–differential tradition. The two traditions were often seen as incompatible because the former emphasizes understanding variation across stimuli or experimental conditions, whereas the latter emphasizes understanding variation across individuals. Cronbach (1957) pointed out that the two traditions are not necessarily incompatible, and he invited psychologists to develop theory and research that would combine the two traditions. My early work (e.g., Sternberg, 1977, 1983) was one of several different attempts to forge the way toward such a synthesis. In other works, I also have sought syntheses. For example, my work on thinking styles (Sternberg, 1997b; Sternberg, Grigorenko, & Zhang, 2008) in some ways has provided a bridge between personality and cognition research. And my work on creativity has integrated aspects of cognitive, personality, and motivational research (e.g., Sternberg, 2010b; Sternberg & Lubart, 1995).

For example, I have proposed a theory of intelligence that posits three abilities (analytical, creative, and practical abilities; Sternberg, 1985,

1997a, 2003, 2010a), and Howard Gardner (1999, 2011) has proposed a theory that posits eight intelligences (linguistic, logical–mathematical, spatial, musical, bodily–kinesthetic, naturalist, interpersonal, and intra-personal). At first glance, the two theories appear to be incompatible: Which is it, three or eight? But the theories also can be viewed as compatible and as analyzing intelligence at different levels. In particular, analytical, creative, and practical processing can be applied in any of the domains of Gardner's theory. For example, one can analyze a poem, write a poem, or read a poem so as to communicate its message—examples of analytical, creative, and practical processing applied in the linguistic domain.

Very often, one will have to negotiate various things with other people—with advisers, with chairs of departments, with journal editors, with colleagues. Sometimes the demands of one person seem utterly incom-patible with the demands of another person. In my experience, however, constructive negotiations often reveal that all parties to an apparent conflict can be satisfied, at least to a first order of approximation. One should not assume that what one party wants cannot be made compatible with what another wants, even if initially the demands or desires seem incompatible.

Very early in my career, I saw myself as a sort of crusader against certain psychometric methods that were being used to study intelligence. I believed that I had better cognitive methods. Later in my career, I real-ized that my methods were not really better, but rather, just different. The best way to study intelligence was to combine the psychometric methods I had rejected with the cognitive methods that I developed. Ideas that had originally seemed incompatible to me—as though one had to adopt one set of ideas or the other set—actually were quite compatible, and were stronger in combination than when considered separately.

THINK FOR YOURSELF: *What are two ideas in psychology that seem, on their surface, incompatible but that might be capable of integration at a deeper level?*

Put It Into Practice: *When you disagree with others, do you look for some kind of synthesis of their point of view with yours? Or do you at least try to understand how they could have come to their point of view? Are there things you could do better to understand how others think?*

Lesson 78
Use Converging Operations

Converging operations refers to the use of multiple methodologies for studying a single psychological phenomenon or problem. The term was first introduced by Garner, Hake, and Eriksen (1956) in a path-breaking article on psychological methodology. The basic idea is that any one operation is, in all likelihood, inadequate for the comprehensive study of any psychological phenomenon. The reason is that any methodology introduces biases of one kind or another, and often, of multiple kinds. By using multiple converging methodologies (i.e., converging operations) for the study of a single psychological phenomenon or problem, one averages over sources of bias.

Many examples show how converging operations can illuminate phenomena in a way that no one operation can. (See the aforementioned Garner et al., 1956, article for some such examples.) Often, new constructs are especially well served by such operations (Sternberg & Grigorenko, 2007).

An example of the need for converging operations can be seen in the study and measurement of intelligence and related intellectual abilities. My colleagues and I (Sternberg, Jarvin, & Grigorenko, 2009) drew on experimental, factor-analytic, cross-cultural, and survey studies, among other types, to analyze the nature of intellectual giftedness. We believed (and I continue to believe) that complex phenomena need to be understood in terms of multiple paradigms of investigation, whether one is studying giftedness or anything else.

If, as Garner et al. (1956) claimed, converging operations are so superior to single operations, why do some and perhaps many psychologists rely largely or even exclusively on a single method of analysis (or, for that matter, only two methods of analysis)? I (Sternberg & Grigorenko, 2007) believe there are three main reasons, none of them really acceptable from a research standpoint.

The first reason is education. Psychologists may have been educated largely in the use of a single methodology. They may have invested heavily in that methodology in their work. Learning how to do structural equation modeling or neural imaging or qualitative analysis, for example, can require a large amount of work, especially if one wishes to perfect one's use of each set of techniques. Researchers may seek to maximize the return on their time investment and use what they have learned as much as possible. Even if they come to see the flaws of their preferred methodology, they may come to view the time invested as a sunken cost and seek to justify or even redeem the investment anyway. They thereby can become fixed in their use of single methods.

The second reason involves the notion of panaceas. Researchers can come to view a single methodology as representing a kind of panacea for the study of a certain problem or set of problems. At one time, some psychometric investigators saw exploratory factor analysis in this way, until its limitations became increasingly apparent (e.g., the existence of an infinite number of rotations of axes, all of which represent equally legitimate solutions statistically). To some of the same investigators, as well as to other investigators, confirmatory factor analysis or structural equation modeling may have come to seem to be panaceas, although these methods also have their limitations, such as reliance on individual differences. Today, some scientists are viewing neural imaging methods as a panacea. Some are busy compiling mental atlases that link certain areas of the brain to certain aspects of cognitive processing, often oblivious to the functional relations between the two and sometimes in the absence of an adequate theoretical foundation (see Sternberg, 2000). The truth is that no method will provide a panacea: Different methods have different advantages and disadvantages, and by using multiple methods one capitalizes on the strengths of the methods while helping to minimize the effects of their weaknesses.

The third reason involves norms. Norms of a field may also lead to methodological fixation. Some years ago, I submitted an article to one of the most prestigious psychological journals available. I was asked to revise the article, replacing regression analyses of the phenomenon under investigation with analyses-of-variance. The request was odd because the two methods of analysis give equivalent information (see Cohen & Cohen, 2002). But the norm of the journal was use of analysis-of-variance reporting, so I had to change my form of reporting. Fields, journals, and other collectivities develop norms that, to the members of those collectivities, may seem perfectly reasonable and even beyond question. These norms may become presuppositions of behavior that are accepted in a rather mindless way (Langer, 2014). The norms may lead investigators to do things in a certain way not because it is the best way but, rather, because it comes to be perceived as the only way or the only way worth pursuing. Norms should support, not undermine, converging operations.

THINK FOR YOURSELF: *Why do many researchers tend to identify themselves with certain methods of investigation rather than branching out and studying psychological phenomena using multiple methods?*

PUT IT INTO PRACTICE: *Why is it better to use multiple methods to study a problem rather than just one method? Are there ways in which you could better use multiple methods, or converging operations, to understand the psychological phenomena in which you are interested?*

Lesson 79
Check Your Work

One of the easiest things you can do is to proofread your work, and few things have a higher payoff for the time invested. Unfortunately, some people just never do it.

Whether you are a student or a professional, few people like to read work that has not been proofread. Professors may give you a lower grade: They have many papers to read and often do not react well to sloppiness or repeated grammatical or other mistakes. Reviewers of articles submitted for publication are even less friendly to poorly presented papers. They are reviewing the papers as a service to the field, not because they have to review them. So they often react negatively when they are repaid for their generosity by a poorly written or badly mangled paper. I have sometimes refused to read such papers. I have returned them to the editor and said that I did not think it a fair use of my time to correct multiple errors of typography that the author should have corrected. Such errors include not only errors of spelling and grammar but also multiple missing pages of text or word-processing errors whereby one is reading one part of a paper when, suddenly, the text shifts to a totally different part that should have been placed elsewhere.

I thus strongly encourage you to proofread all your work, as I have proofread this manuscript. Proofreading does not guarantee that you will fix all errors. Sometimes you can look at an error multiple times and not see it, simply because it is your error. But, in general, you will do yourself and your reputation a favor if you are careful about your work.

When I suggest you proofread your work, I am talking about proof-reading "within reason." A real career-killer is super perfectionism. Some people are never ready to let go of anything. They need to proofread their work, and then revise and proofread it again, and then keep revising and proofreading it, just to make sure. By the time they get around to sending a paper out for publication, someone else has already beaten them to the punch and done something similar. It is important to proofread your work, but not to the point of obsession. Find the golden mean. Do not hang on to things so long that by the time you let go of them they have lost much of their value.

◨ ◨ ◨ ◨ ◨ ◨ ◨

THINK FOR YOURSELF: *How would you feel if you were a reviewer for a journal, who was not being paid for his or her work, and you received an article to review that was full of typographical errors that the author of the article simply did not trouble him- or herself to correct?*

PUT IT INTO PRACTICE: *Do you proofread your work before you submit it? Do you know that there probably is no one thing you can do more easily and more quickly that will improve the quality of your work?*

Lesson 80
Ask Colleagues for Informal Comments on Your Work

Related to the notion of proofreading is the notion of seeking informal feedback. I have found, countless times, that colleagues will discover errors, even blatant errors that I never would have noticed in my work. Sometimes the errors are ones that I would have been downright embarrassed for others to have noticed. Other times I have not sought informal collegial feedback and have regretted it when I received negative comments from reviewers that I am certain could have been avoided had I first gotten informal feedback.

When you hear your voice on a recording medium, it often does not sound like you. It sounds like someone else speaking. Which is the way your voice sounds, the way you hear it or the way it sounds when recorded? The way it sounds when recorded, of course. Because you are both speaking and listening, there is a distortion in what you hear. The same is true when you do work. Because you both write it and evaluate it, there is bound to be some degree of distortion. Others can help you get through this distortion and see things you never would see if left to your own devices.

I once wrote a reply to a critique of my work. I did not see it at the time, but my reply was ill-tempered. Fortunately, a colleague of mine did see it and discouraged me from submitting for publication a rebuttal that would have been, in a word, embarrassing. Get informal feedback—it may save you from yourself!

▣ ▣ ▣ ▣ ▣ ▣ ▣

THINK FOR YOURSELF: *Why are scholars often reluctant to ask colleagues for comments on their work?*

PUT IT INTO PRACTICE: *Do you seek out informal feedback on your work? From whom? If not, from whom might you seek it out?*

Lesson 81

Ask About the Best and Worst Possible Outcomes Before You Even Begin

Sometimes students or colleagues come to me with ideas that do not seem very appealing. But I recognize that the fact that an idea does not seem appealing to me means nothing more than that—namely, that it is not appealing to me. Others, perhaps many others, may love the idea. When I am skeptical about an idea, say, for a research project, I sometimes ask the colleague or student what he or she views as the best and worst possible outcomes of the proposed work. If the success of the entire project would yield only a single test of statistical significance, for example, the individual might want to think carefully about investing major amounts of time or resources, especially if no strong evidence indicates that the test will come out the way one hopes it will.

I personally do not like all-or-nothing kinds of projects and try to avoid them. By an *all-or-nothing project*, I mean one that either comes out exactly the way I had hoped for or is a loss. I try to build features into studies so that if one thing does not work out, something else may. For example, I may add additional dependent variables so that if the first dependent variable does not yield significant results, another one may. Or I may add an independent variable so that if I do not get a main effect I hoped for, I may nevertheless get an interaction.

The stakes are different at different points in a career. If you are tenured, you probably can take larger risks more easily than if you are not. In any case, you always need to look at the cost–benefit ratio for the projects you undertake, and if the costs are especially great, consider whether the benefits outweigh them.

One kind of risk you never should take is an ethical one. Do not count on not getting caught. Tolerance for ethical lapses in all areas of academia and in society in general is extremely low. For example, lapses in following human subjects protocols that at one time might have been tolerated and largely ignored, today are noticed and dealt with.

In making all these points, I should make one thing clear again, as I have before: I am not claiming to be perfect—far from it. I have made many mistakes, perhaps more than my share. But we all need to learn from experience, and I have tried to do so.

THINK FOR YOURSELF: *What is an example of a disaster that someone you know (including yourself) has encountered that might have been avoided by thinking in advance of the worst possible outcome?*

PUT IT INTO PRACTICE: *When you undertake a new project, do you ask yourself what the best possible and worst possible outcomes are? If not, why not?*

Lesson 82
Sometimes the Reason We Start Doing Things Is Not the Reason We Continue Doing Them

I once was talking with a colleague who had emigrated from the United States and had gone to live abroad. I asked him whether he had fulfilled his goals in moving—if the move had brought him whatever it was he was seeking. He commented that the reasons one went to live in another country often were not the reasons one decided to stay, and that one had to decide, having lived there for a number of years, whether it was a good move or a not so good one. Those who decided it was a not so good one either lived in a state of dissatisfaction or went back to the United States.

It occurred to me that his comments were a good lesson that applied in many contexts. Often the reasons for which we undertake the things we do in our careers are not the reasons for which we continue to do them. For example, when I became director of graduate studies in psychology when I was a professor at Yale, I accepted the job merely to serve the department. I initially had little or no interest in it. But after doing it for a while, I discovered I actually enjoyed it because it was a chance to help graduate students. I continued it not just out of a sense of service but also out of a sense of purpose and personal meaning.

I think that flexibility here, as in many things, is of key importance. Research projects sometimes have come out better than I ever thought possible, not because they worked out as I expected but because they worked out in some entirely different way. Being director of graduate studies for our department had some unexpected pains but many unexpected joys. The bottom line is that you need to be continually reassessing what you are doing and why you are doing it, and make the most of the opportunities available to you.

THINK FOR YOURSELF: *What are some of the reasons people continue to do things they initially thought they would like to do even after they discover that what they are doing is not something they really want to do?*

PUT IT INTO PRACTICE: *When was the last time you seriously reassessed what you are doing in your work? If it is time for a reassessment, what do you conclude? Are the original reasons you undertook the work you are doing still valid?*

V
Job and Career

Lesson 83
Be Proactive, Not Reactive

There is a kind of person who almost never makes money in the stock market: This is the person who waits to see where others are investing and then follows them. For example, he or she will eagerly buy the investment newsletter for a particular year, find out who the winners of last year's mutual funds investment derby were, and then buy shares in that mutual fund. The next year, of course, the fund will almost never do as well (a data point that could be predicted by statistical regression alone). By following the pack, he or she somehow almost always manages to come out with the short end of the stick.

Professional lives show the same trends. There is a large group of people who are always waiting to see who jumps in what pool, and then they jump in after several people whom they admire jump in first. By the time they jump in, however, the pool is crowded, not so clear, and perhaps even dirty! The people who are merely reactive rarely come out well ahead.

When students arrive on campus—starting as an undergraduate student, a graduate student, a postdoctoral student, or even, sometimes, as a faculty member—one of the biggest mistakes I've seen them make is to wait for things to happen. They arrive and expect that the university will provide some series of stimuli, that they will respond to these stimuli, and that by doing so properly, they will be on the path toward greatness. Nothing could be further from the truth. What a university does, typically, is to provide an environment in which resources and opportunities are there for the asking. But more often than not, the opportunities do not just come to you. Rather, you must seek them out. And often you must create the opportunities. In other words, you need to be proactive rather than reactive.

I ran for president of the American Psychological Association twice. The first time I was reactive. I waited for things to happen. They didn't—other than my losing. The second time I was proactive. I created a campaign, with the help of my friends and colleagues. Everyone worked together with a common goal. I—or really, we as a group—won. The lesson was simple: Good things do not come to those who wait. Good things come to those who go after good things and make them happen. Decide what you want, then go for it. Don't wait for it to come to you.

In being proactive, keep in mind the expression to be careful of what you wish for. At one time I applied for a grant from a source that had a reputation for being difficult to work with. I received the grant and spent the next few years regretting it because all I got from the funders was grief. So be proactive, but be sure that what you are proactive for is what you really want.

THINK FOR YOURSELF: *Do you think rewards in life tend to go to those who tend to be proactive or to those who tend to be reactive? Why?*

PUT IT INTO PRACTICE: *Are you waiting for things to happen, or are you making them happen? Are you actively working to improve yourself and your work, or are you just hoping that it somehow will happen? When you are anxious about something not working out, do you focus on your anxiety or on making things work out?*

Lesson 84
Turn Defeats Into Opportunities

There inevitably come times in one's career when one experiences what seem like major defeats. As I mentioned above, it is important not to give up. But it is surprising how many times a defeat can be turned into an opportunity if one is willing to use the defeat as a lesson for the future.

The first major defeat I had was pretty early—when I took the introductory psychology course. I was eager to major in psychology because I had done poorly on intelligence tests as a child and I wanted to understand what intelligence was and, hence, why I had done so poorly. So I figured that a psychology major would answer the question for me, and then maybe I could spend my life researching intelligence.

The course did not go well, to say the least. I got a grade of "C" in the course. I was always awful in courses that emphasized straight rote recall, and this course came pretty close to that. Indeed, things went poorly from the start. The professor gave us our first test—actually, it was the first test I took as an undergraduate at Yale—and then, a few days later, handed back the tests with the understanding that we could leave for the Thanksgiving holiday as soon as we got our test paper back. To make matters worse, he handed back the tests in descending order. The test was on a 10-point scale, so he first handed back the 10s, then the 9s, then the 8s, and so on. The scores went down, and I eventually came to the conclusion that my paper must have gotten out of order. I might not have gotten a 10, but when he was down past the 7s, it was clear that something was very wrong.

Eventually, the only people left in the room were people who I assumed were not in the psychology course to become great psychologists—and me. Finally, the professor handed me back my test paper, with a "3" written at the top. The professor commented, "There is a famous Sternberg in psychology and it is obvious from your test score that there won't be another one." What a bummer!

My Thanksgiving vacation left me feeling that I did not have much to give thanks for. It was clear that I was not making it in psychology and would have to find another field. After completing the course with the "C," I decided to switch my major to mathematics, another interest of mine. In the second semester, I took an introductory course for mathematics majors, and failed the midterm. The mathematics professor suggested that those who had scored below 40 on the midterm drop the course. As I had scored in the mid-30s, I dropped. I decided to switch back to psychology, as a "C" seemed better than an "F."

I decided to turn my defeat into an opportunity: I was going to show the professor—and myself—that I could succeed in psychology. My subsequent grades in psychology were mostly "A"s, except for the physiological psychology course, which also required a great deal of memorization. Moreover, I realized that many people do not learn well from courses that emphasize rote memory, and this defeat became a basis for much of my later work on the psychology of instruction. Thus, my experience motivated me not only to improve my own work in psychology but also to research and develop ways that would help other people to learn better.

The humiliations do not end as one grows older. Later in my career, after I had received an endowed chair, I was invited by the undergraduate psychology organization at Yale to give a talk to a group of undergraduate psychology majors. Of course, I was happy to accept their invitation. I went on the assigned day at the assigned time and was greeted by the two women who had organized the talk, plus one other individual—someone who was visiting my research group at Yale. Thus, I had a total of one person who was to be in the audience. The undergraduates were very apologetic and said that perhaps their publicity efforts had not been all they could have been. I told them not to worry—that in fact, it was perfectly fine.

What I said was that this experience would be invaluable to me in the future. In the future, if I went to give a talk, and as few as two people showed up, then I would at least have done twice as well as I had done that day. In other words, I doubted I would ever again feel that I had an insufficiently large audience. From time to time, I give a talk and not so many people show up. I remember back to that day and think that as long as I have more than one person, I'm doing better than I did that day.

When I started as a professor at Cornell in Ithaca, New York, I was somewhat depressed by how far away it was from the places to which I was used to going. Even New York City is a serious 4.5 hours away. I felt defeated: Any time I wanted to travel, it seemed to be a big deal. But then I realized something: I had young children (4-year-old triplets), and, in the past, I kept feeling like I was not seeing them enough. I was afraid they would grow up and I would hardly get to be with them. The silver lining in the distance from other places is that now I only accept trips I really want to take. What had seemed like a defeat now seems like a victory: I now have the opportunity to spend the time with my young children that I always wanted to spend with them.

In short, the question is not whether you will have defeats; you will. The question is whether you can learn from them and turn them into victories. In many cases, you can. It is up to you to figure out how. You usually need a Plan B, in your career and in life. So as you plan to do a project, simultaneously be thinking about what you will do if that project does not work out as you had hoped.

In my career, my greatest self-perceived defeat happened when I was fairly far along. I did not get renewed funding on a grant that was really important to me and to my program of research. For a while, I felt like I essentially could throw in the towel on my research career. My most important project was out of money. I then decided to try to turn the defeat into an opportunity. I went into administration for 8 years to put my ideas on this program of research into practice. The ideas in fact worked remarkably well in practice. I then returned, after this stint, to being a professor. There are opportunities, sometimes, even in what seem to be the most humiliating defeats.

231

▣ ▣ ▣ ▣ ▣ ▣ ▣

THINK FOR YOURSELF: *What exactly counts
as a defeat in life?*

PUT IT INTO PRACTICE: *Have you had any of what you
considered to be major defeats in your life? Did you find
opportunity in the defeat? Are you afraid of any defeats
in your immediate future? If so, do you have a Plan B
to turn the defeat into a potential opportunity?*

Lesson 85
Create Opportunities and Take Advantage of Them When They Arise

Some years ago I realized that I felt that I was in a rut. I felt as though my research was moving in a direction different from that of my department, and I was thinking that it was time for a change. I had an offer from another university and was considering leaving my position.

At the same time, my research group was in a particularly favorable position. We had just gotten a couple of large grants, and so were at an especially good time for initiating new research projects. I talked to a high-level administrator at the university that had offered me a job about the possibility of my starting a center on abilities, but somehow the idea had not quite clicked with him. He was not oppositional but did not seem to understand exactly what I wanted. Maybe that was because I was not sure of exactly what I wanted. I then spoke with some high-level administrators at my home institution, and they offered to give me space in another building, as my group had outgrown the space I had in the psychology department. We had a choice of buildings, and I immediately picked an old historical house at the north end of the campus.

Basically, I did what I found one must do throughout one's entire career: Create opportunities. No one came to me and suggested I start a center. I saw a possibility, and with the collaboration of many invaluable colleagues, realized it. At any point in your career, you can create opportunities or wait for opportunities to come to you. I find that opportunities rarely come to you, although they sometimes do. The name of the game is to create opportunities, rather than waiting for them magically to appear.

Although one often must create opportunities, there are times when, almost out of nowhere, opportunities do arise. Some people take them; others let them go. The important thing is, if they are the right opportunities, to take them when they arise.

Some years ago, I received a phone call out of the blue asking me whether I would be interested in formulating a program for helping Venezuelan schoolchildren to develop their intellectual skills. I knew virtually nothing about Venezuela, did not speak a word of Spanish, and had little idea of how in the world I or anyone else could create a successful program to improve intellectual skills. But I recognized I was getting an opportunity that I probably would get only one time in my career. I grabbed it. I learned about Venezuela and its new Ministry for the Development of Intelligence, I learned Spanish (which I now speak fluently), and I thought long and hard about how to create a program to develop intellectual skills.

Many good things came out of my accepting the offer. I got to visit Venezuela several times and learn about the culture. I learned a new language (when I was in my early 30s) and have had many opportunities to use it over the course of my life. I created the Intelligence Applied program (Sternberg, 1986). And I made many new friends. Things did not end as well as they might have. The government that offered me and others the chance to develop programs lost in the next election, and the programs were quickly dismantled. Indeed, the opposing party ran under a platform of making fun of the programs and saying that they were just a big waste of money. As a result of the election loss, I never got to evaluate that particular program. But I'm glad I took the opportunity when it arose, and I would not have given it up for anything.

I have been editor of two journals of the American Psychological Association (APA) and one of the Association for Psychological Science. Each time I became editor, I tried to make substantive and meaningful changes in the journal. Each time I was president of an APA division, I tried to do something that would leave a lasting impact on the division. I may or may not have succeeded. But I did not want to let opportunities for meaningful change go by the wayside. Some people take offices for little more than what appears to be the purpose of putting the offices on their vitas. In one particularly egregious case, a colleague I know became president of an APA division and simply disappeared. No one could get in touch with him. He apparently cared about getting the office, not about doing anything with it. The past president essentially had to run the division for that year. Most people are not so crassly opportunistic. But people who blow opportunities often do it not just for themselves but for others, as was the case for the individual who ran for the division presidency, won, and then proceeded to do nothing. The division deserved better, and so, perhaps, did the individual. After this, few people in the division wanted to have anything to do with him.

Many opportunities have come up during the course of my career: the opportunity to edit journals, the opportunity to be president of APA divisions, the opportunity to serve on various committees doing what I believed to be important work. In almost anyone's life, good opportunities come from time to time. Don't let them go!

At the same time, realize that not all opportunities will pan out as you had hoped. I once wrote a grant proposal that looked, to me, like the basis for very promising research. The proposal was funded. The research did not pan out. At the end of the funding period, what we had to show for our research was a failure to replicate our earlier findings. Honestly, it was pretty depressing—all those person-hours spent in a failure to replicate. The failure to replicate showed us that the findings we had were not as robust as we had hoped for, nothing one hopes to find! So grab those opportunities, but do not expect at the end of every trail is a pot of gold. New opportunities are always a gamble. Many will work out, but some will not. And that's the way life is: Nothing ventured, nothing gained.

One of the best ways to create opportunities is to surround yourself with smart, eager, enthusiastic people. At various times in your life, you may have the choice between being with people who are great at what they do or with people who are not so great. The better opportunities are almost always with the people who are great. You have more to learn from them than from people who are not as expert as you. In the short run, surrounding yourself with mediocre people may raise your self-esteem. But in the long run, you will lose opportunities to grow that only great colleagues can provide.

So how do you create opportunities for yourself? Be open to new research collaborations. Teach new courses that may give you new ideas. Run for office in a professional association. Offer to review articles for a journal or even to be consulting editor, if you are senior enough. Offer to serve on interesting university committees. Don't wait for opportunities to come to you. Seek them out!

THINK FOR YOURSELF: *What is the problem with waiting for opportunity to knock at your door?*

PUT IT INTO PRACTICE: *Do you actively seek out opportunities, or do you hope that they will just come to you? What kinds of concrete, proactive steps could you take to create more opportunities for yourself?*

Lesson 86
You Can Go Very Far on Reflective Hard Work

My graduate adviser, Gordon Bower, used to say that what matters in a career is "throughput," or how much you get done. There are many ways to increase your throughput, but there is no substitute for hard work.

A successful academic career does not come easily. Virtually everyone I know who is successful in academia has worked very hard. They may not show that they work hard, and they may even hide it. But they work hard, nevertheless. It does not matter whether they are the sharpest knife in the drawer or one of the blunter ones: Hard work is almost a sine qua non for success.

You want not only to work hard but also to work smart. You need to think carefully about where you invest your resources. There will be many demands on your time. If you are going to work hard, then make sure you work hard on those things that are meaningful to you and will get you where you want to go.

Ericsson (1996, 2009) has argued that the not-so-secret secret of becoming an expert is deliberate practice—working hard at a task in a focused, deliberative, and reflective way. You become an expert writer by writing a lot, and by working to improve your writing while you are doing it. You become an expert teacher by teaching a lot, and by asking yourself how you can improve your teaching. If you want to become an expert at whatever you do, work hard at it, and continually ask yourself how you can get better. But remember one thing: Hard work on a project will count for little or

Psychology 101½: The Unspoken Rules for Success in Academia, Second Edition, by R. J. Sternberg
Copyright © 2017 by the American Psychological Association. All rights reserved.

nothing if you do not finish the project. I have seen any number of students work hard on a project, only to abandon it midstream. Such hard work is not productive because it fails to yield a tangible product. Hard work does not always have to yield a tangible product, but it sure helps if it does!

Just playing music over and over again does not make you play it better. Indeed, if you do not pay attention to what you are doing, you may end up just reinforcing your old mistakes. It is the same with work in psychology. You need to work hard, but always ask yourself how you can improve at what you are doing.

Hard work is probably necessary but not sufficient for success. I once thought I had what it took to be a pretty good cellist. I worked pretty hard at it—for a while. But I did not seem to be on the way to becoming a pro. So then I stopped working as hard at it. Effort and talent are very closely intertwined. Many times, if we find we do not have the talent for something, we do not try as hard to succeed at it. So we do less deliberate practice, but because of our perception that what we are doing is not one of our great strengths.

If you stop working hard at something, just make sure that it truly is because you lack talent. When I was younger, my French teacher told me I lacked talent for foreign languages. I never took another foreign-language course in high school or college. Later in my life, when I needed to learn Spanish, I started studying Spanish with a tutor. My tutor told me I had unusual talent for foreign languages. The difference? The match between the way the two teachers taught and the way I learned. Sometimes you may think you lack talent for something, when in fact you lack talent only for the way that something is being taught. Make sure, therefore, that if something is meaningful to you, you give it your best try before giving up on it. In my case, I found that hard work really could get me far in learning foreign languages.

□ □ □ □ □ □

THINK FOR YOURSELF: *Western societies tend more to emphasize ability, whereas Eastern societies tend more to emphasize effort. Might Eastern societies have an idea from which Western societies could and should learn?*

Put It Into Practice: *Do you give up easily? If so, how could you convince yourself to try harder at what you do? Do you let people discourage you from pursuing your interests? How could you show others, and yourself, that working hard at those interests could help you achieve positive results?*

Lesson 87

Balance Long-Term Goals With Short-Term Goals

One of the problems you face when you are starting out a career is how to balance the long term with the short term. On the one hand, long-term projects are often those that have the potential to make the most difference to a field. On the other hand, promotion and tenure decisions come upon one quickly, and if one does not have anything to show on one's vita, one can end up being in serious trouble.

I decided early in my career to use an "asset-allocation" plan. I would do some long-term projects that I was particularly interested in, but at the same time that I would do some things that were shorter term so that, in the short run, I would not be stuck without anything to show for my time as a faculty member. That strategy generally has served me well during my career. Have some long-term projects that may be high-payoff ones, but be sure as well to have some shorter term projects that you are pretty sure to get published, even if they are not going to be the world-shakers that put your name on the map.

I have seen other faculty members (and corporation executives, and many others!) go entirely for the short term. I believe that such a mentality is mistaken. One may end up with more to show in the short run but make little of a lasting contribution in the long run. One assistant professor in my department was publishing away in his early years, and even getting the articles into very good journals. But the projects were short term and bite sized, and they have been little cited. In the short term, he accumulated many publications and a long vita. In the long term, the work seems to have had little impact. You need to think both for the short and the long terms. You cannot ignore the short term, because often you have things you need to accomplish and do not have much time in which to accomplish them. But you cannot ignore the long term, because the long-term things are likely to make the most difference.

As a very senior person in the field, I have found that when one looks back on a career, the long-term goals are the ones I remember and cherish. I had a lot of short-term goals along the way; I've forgotten almost all of them. So focus on some truly long-term goals because those are the ones that will make your life meaningful. As an example, I never thought, when I was in my 20s and very career focused, that the long-term goal that would mean the most to me has turned out to be raising a family. I hope that my work will live on past me; I know that my family—my five children and their children—will live on way after I'm gone.

THINK FOR YOURSELF: *Why do people often tend to put more attention in their lives toward fulfillment of short-term than long-term goals?*

PUT IT INTO PRACTICE: *What are your long-term goals? Do you have a plan to reach them? What is it? Do you also have short-term goals that will help get you to the long-term goals? How will they help you get to where you want to go?*

Lesson 88
Spread Yourself Neither too Thin nor too Thick

Because there are so many demands on your time in an academic career, you will find more and more to do as your career advances further and further. You may find yourself with teaching obligations; administrative responsibilities; one or more research projects; writing articles and perhaps grant proposals; doing outside activities, such as consulting; reviewing papers or grant proposals; informally advising students and colleagues; and so forth. And, of course, you have personal responsibilities as well! One of the joys of an academic career is the diversity it affords. In 40 years, I've never been bored, because there is always so much to do. At the same time, I've seen many academics who fall prey to the trap of spreading themselves too thin. They try to do too much and end up getting little done. I had one colleague who was involved in more projects than anyone could count, including the colleague herself, but who never seemed to finish any of them. The result was that her career did not go as she wished, and she antagonized people who expected work from her that never quite seemed to get done.

Spreading yourself too thin has several disadvantages. First, work you need to get done doesn't get done because you have too many other things to do. Second, you may disappoint others who expect work of you that you fail to complete in a timely manner. Third, you may give others the impression of being scattered or flighty. Finally, when it comes time to be evaluated, you may be disappointed with the result. Whereas you may feel like you've done a lot, you may find others criticizing your lack of productivity because so little got done.

I must admit that I have a tendency to spread myself too thin. No reason to keep it a secret, because anyone who knows me will say the same thing. So I try to build in safeguards. For example, I usually review articles I receive quickly. But if I am busy and they start to accumulate, I start turning down new reviews after I have three reviews waiting to be done.

My worst venture into spreading myself too thin occurred during my sophomore year of college. In the spring of 1971, I took a course load that was totally ridiculous, just to show myself I could do it. Well, I couldn't. I was way overcommitted and was on the path toward disaster. Totally by chance, I lucked out. That spring, during the height of the Vietnam War, there was a national student strike. As a result, the requirements for some of my courses were reduced and we all were allowed to take incomplete grades in our courses. The strike saved me. But I don't expect any similar events in the future, so I try hard not to overcommit myself.

The complementary mistake is to spread yourself too thick—to do too few things but try to do them in great depth. There is a great temptation in academia to do very little but to do it to the extreme. For example, some people devote all their time to their research but neglect their teaching, or they become so absorbed in teaching that they neglect their research. They just do not take care of all their responsibilities. Spreading yourself too thick, like spreading yourself too thin, has adverse consequences. When you come up for evaluation, it likely will seem like your evaluators are targeting you not for what you did but for what you did not do. People often get by—at least in many university settings—if they make sure they cover all their bases, at least to some extent. Almost no one will expect you to be a super teacher, a super researcher, and a super administrator too. But you probably will be expected to be at least adequate at all three, and perhaps to excel in one (or possibly two). If you leave one base totally uncovered, it is not only the base but also you who will be exposed to potential grief.

The same principle that applies across areas of endeavor applies within an area of endeavor. For example, in teaching, you may be expected to be at least decent at different kinds of teaching (e.g., lectures, seminars, one-on-one mentoring). If you do at least a reasonable job of all three, then you can probably afford to be better at one (e.g., seminars) and not as good at the others. But again, it pays to have your bases covered. Similarly, in research, you need to pay attention to many things—the theoretical background, who the participants are and how many of them you have, what materials you use and how well they sample the domain they are supposed to sample, and so on. Failing to pay attention to any one aspect of a study can result in the study's being rejected just because that one aspect was neglected.

In sum, spread yourself neither too thick nor too thin. Try to allocate your resources carefully. Find the right way to divide your time, and then stick with it.

THINK FOR YOURSELF: *How do you decide what the right balance is between spreading yourself too thick or too thin?*

PUT IT INTO PRACTICE: *Do you spread yourself too thin? Too thick? How can you change your behavior to make your commitments consistent with time and effort you have available to devote to what you need to do?*

Lesson 89
Specialize, but Not to the Point of Losing the Forest for the Trees

Some scholars like to move from one topic to the next, others like to dig into one topic and stay with it indefinitely. In my experience, going to either extreme is a mistake.

If you move very quickly from one topic to another to another, you are likely to be viewed as flighty. When people in a given field are asked to evaluate you, they may think that you have done little because they know only or primarily your work in that field. Such a superficial approach to problems is generally devalued in the field of psychology. Departments are often reluctant to hire or retain people who are viewed as superficial.

Although the rewards of the field tend to be for depth, my own personal opinion is that some people can carry depth too far. They start working on one problem and then never leave it. I think an analogy of research (and often, of teaching and administrative work) to a goldmine is apt. Usually, when you first start mining gold from a given mine, you do not find the richest veins. Eventually, by careful planning and follow-through, you do find these richest veins. Then, after a point, the mine starts to become exhausted and the gold it has to yield more and more elusive. Part of any career is knowing when to move on.

In graduate school, there may be a temptation to become specialized very early. Fight it! Graduate school is your chance to learn broadly as well as deeply. Don't become an overspecialized grind before you even start your career. Ensure that you get a broad enough education so that later,

Psychology 101½: The Unspoken Rules for Success in Academia, Second Edition, by R. J. Sternberg
Copyright © 2017 by the American Psychological Association. All rights reserved.

if you want to change research areas, you do not find yourself clueless as to how to learn anything outside your original field of specialization.

It is for this reason that, for example, terms as editor of a journal tend to be fixed, as do terms as chair of a psychology department. After a while, new blood is needed. Journals in which the same person stays as editor for an indefinite term show, in my opinion, signs of exhaustion. And younger people are deprived of a chance to contribute their editorial skills. Similarly, research areas tend to yield only so much gold. As a research area becomes more and more mature, the amount of interesting new information per article in that area often starts to decrease. Research areas are not abandoned, for the most part, because all the questions in them are answered. On the contrary, few questions in psychology are ever answered for good! Rather, they are abandoned because they become boring. But there are, in any field, people who seem incapable of being bored, and they often find themselves doing more and more that interests other people less and less. It therefore is important to know when to move on.

Another reason not to overspecialize is that, sooner or later, we exhaust any project or set of projects on which we work. To remain creative, we need to move on to study something else. If you are overspecialized, it will be harder to think of new kinds of projects because you just won't be able to see beyond the kind of project you are working on. If you think more broadly, you will be able to jump from one tree to the next, or even one forest to the next, and maintain your creativity in a new avenue of work.

So I believe it is worthwhile to find a middle ground between overspecialization, where you work on just one problem or in just one narrow area, and underspecialization, in which you are a jack of all trades but a master of none. You will have the most satisfying career, I believe, if you are focused but versatile and willing to try out new things.

THINK FOR YOURSELF: *What leads people to lose the forest for the trees—to get so lost in the details that they miss the point of what they are doing?*

PUT IT INTO PRACTICE: *Are you continually learning about new areas of endeavor, or do you find yourself stuck learning more and more about the same old same old? Or do you find yourself learning about so many things that you lose focus on any one? What is the best way to find a middle ground?*

Lesson 90
If You Do It Well, You'll Most Likely Do It Again

Years ago, I accepted a job as associate editor of the journal *Child Development*. I thought I did a reasonable job of it. Perhaps I did, because soon thereafter I was asked to be associate editor of a second journal (*Intelligence*). Then I became editor of a journal (*Psychological Bulletin*) and after that of still another journal (*Contemporary Psychology: APA Review of Books*). Now I'm editor of *Perspectives on Psychological Science*. Of course, my whole career does not follow this pattern. About 10 years ago, I was on a university committee for choosing assistant professors to win special university fellowships in the social sciences. I showed up for what I thought was the meeting and was surprised to see that I did not know anyone at the meeting. The reason was that I was at the wrong meeting: My committee had met the week before, and I had been a no-show. For quite a while after the no-show event, I was not asked to serve on any committees. I did not have to wonder why. I learned my lesson, and now double-check dates and times of meetings.

There is an expression "No good deed goes unpunished": If the university (or anyone else) finds out that you do something particularly well, you can expect to be asked to do it again and again. It therefore behooves you to ask yourself, in taking on a new responsibility, not only what the responsibility is, but where it is likely to lead you.

Psychology 101½: The Unspoken Rules for Success in Academia, Second Edition, by R. J. Sternberg Copyright © 2017 by the American Psychological Association. All rights reserved.

In sum, if there is a particular kind of task you like, accept opportunities to do it: You will probably be asked to do it more, if you do a reasonably good job. But if there is a kind of task you do not like to do, beware. If you do it and do a good job, you may end up doing it again and again. When Wendell Garner came to Yale as a faculty member, he came partly because he was sick and tired of being an administrator at Johns Hopkins, and wanted to do something different, namely, be just a regular faculty member. Within a short amount of time, he was department chair, and shortly thereafter, he was selected as dean of the graduate school. He had the misfortune of being good at something he did not particularly like to do and at something many others do not do well. He also had trouble saying no, so he ended up doing administration when he probably would have rather done his research full-time.

THINK FOR YOURSELF: *How can people find things that they both enjoy and are good at?*

PUT IT INTO PRACTICE: *Do you make sure you devote your time, to the extent possible, to things that are meaningful to you? Can you say no to projects that are not right for you? If not, can you change yourself so that you can turn down those projects that are unlikely to lead you where you want to go?*

Lesson 91
Don't Sell Out

As college students, we used to talk about "selling out." Going to college in the late 1960s and early 1970s, we considered selling oneself out to be the ultimate sin. Each of us wanted to be true to himself or herself. Few of us have been. And oddly enough, if one looks at who was true to the goals he or she set, it would have been hard to predict at the time which of us would accomplish that.

There are many different ways of selling out. You can go into a field just for the money, as did many of my friends. Almost all of them today are unhappy and cannot wait until they retire. You can take positions you do not really believe in, just to please others. Once you start on this path, you find yourself on a slippery slope. Eventually, you may have trouble figuring out what you believe in, and others may as well.

The opportunities to sell out start early and continue. In my own case, I have had many opportunities. Some years ago, I found myself in disagreement with a superior over a whole number of issues. The superior was not very happy that I did not like the way he was doing things. Eventually, he must have gotten rather upset, because he said to me that "the train is leaving the station, and you can either get on it or not." The implication was that if I did "not get on the train," he would make my life unpleasant. So I had a choice: Get on his train or risk the consequences. I told him that I was not getting on. I have never regretted sticking to my guns. I did not want to get on his train; it was not the train for me.

I guess my first opportunity to sell myself out came right at the beginning of graduate school. A group of us were linked up with our adviser, and each of us was supposed to say what we were interested in studying. We knew what we thought our adviser wanted to hear: semantic memory, which was what he was studying at the time. The first student in the line said he was interested in studying semantic memory. So did the second and the third. I was up next. My interest was in human intelligence, but no one in the department I was in studied that topic. This was my chance to be true to myself and say "human intelligence." Of course, I'm no cheap sellout, so when my turn came, I said . . . "semantic memory." Yep, I sold myself out. I look back on that event with embarrassment. So far as I know, I've never done it again.

Of course, I, like everyone else, make mistakes in my judgments. I have been involved in search committees that have made hires that later proved to be ill-considered. I have undertaken research projects with confidence, only to have them bomb badly. I have trusted colleagues and employees whom I should not have trusted. But I have found that it is better to act upon what you believe rather than to sell out, even if you later come to the conclusion that your beliefs need to be modified. The challenges never end. Right now, I find myself disagreeing in some ways with the way the educational establishment is moving in the United States. There is more and more emphasis on very high-stakes testing and on testing that I believe to be of a narrow kind. It would be much easier for me simply to go along to get along. But I cannot do it. I am happy to work with people who disagree with me, but I find that I cannot fall silent or capitulate just for the sake of taking the easy way out. I hope you find the same.

Think for Yourself: *Why do some people sell out easily and others never or almost never?*

Put It Into Practice: *Have you sold yourself out in your career? Was it worth it? If so, exactly what did you gain? If not, how could you stop yourself from doing it again so that in the future you are true to yourself?*

Lesson 92
Luck Seems To Come in Streaks— Both Bad and Good

Gilovich, Vallone, and Tversky (1985) studied what is sometimes called the "hot-hand" phenomenon—the tendency for athletes, such as basketball players, to have runs of good luck. They found out that the runs are in the eyes of the beholders: They are not real. In your career, you may find—as I have—that luck does seem to run in streaks. I have gone through periods in which almost every grant proposal I wrote got funded and I felt that I had finally hit my stride. Then I have gone through periods in which nothing I wrote got funded—in which it seemed like just putting my name on proposals was enough to doom them. During the dry spells, giving up often seems like the only option.

Sometimes the bad luck is personal. You may have one illness followed by another illness followed by another, or you may lose one important person in your life after another. It seems as though you have been personally selected for bad luck.

Don't give up. Instead, take a look at a table of random numbers. Chances are that you will see many more runs of the same digit than you ever would expect. Why is it that people even need tables of random numbers, or computer-generated strings of random numbers? The reason is that people are absolutely terrible at generating them. They put into their strings far fewer runs than would exist in a string of truly random numbers. So there will be periods when things seem to be up or down very often.

It never lasts forever, any more than the stock market ever stays permanently high or low.

Keep one other thing in mind: We often remember our streaks of bad luck better than we remember our streaks of good luck. So if you are cursing yourself for being in a streak of bad luck, think back. Chances are that you also have had streaks of good luck and just never paid them the same degree of attention.

▣ ▣ ▣ ▣ ▣ ▣ ▣

THINK FOR YOURSELF: *Why do people perceive luck as coming in streaks when, typically, it really does not?*

PUT IT INTO PRACTICE: *Have you ever felt like you have had one or more streaks of bad luck? If so, how have you dealt with them? Is there anything you could do better, recognizing that these streaks do eventually pass, one way or another?*

Lesson 93
Be Patient About
Making a Difference

A major goal I have set for myself is to change the way education is done in the United States. In particular, I believe that the way we educate children in the United States tends to benefit children who are strong in memory and analytical abilities but to place at a disadvantage children whose strengths are in creative and practical abilities.

How far have I gotten toward achieving my goals? Not very far, really. At times I have been terribly frustrated. Here I am, 65 years of age, and I have had very little impact on changing education in the United States. There are days when I wonder why I bother even to try. Then I remember the advice of my undergraduate mentor, Endel Tulving, who once said to me that people tend to vastly underestimate the amount of time it takes to get any meaningful kind of change to take place. His words have kept me going at times when I have felt that my efforts to change education— or anything else—have stalled or even hit a dead end.

When we are young, we often believe that we can change things pretty quickly, if only we set our minds to it. Then we encounter resistance from many quarters, and we may become discouraged that tasks that we thought would be easy are much harder than we ever expected. Often the opposition we encounter seems misguided. For some reason, people don't acknowledge the sublime reasonableness of what we suggest. But remember Tulving's advice. It can take a substantial amount of time even to get fairly simple and straightforward things to change in a positive way. And remember as well that the courses of action that appear reasonable to you may appear to be anything but reasonable to someone else. However my actions may appear to others, I'm determined to make a difference both in my personal and my professional lives and, even at 65, I'm not giving up!

THINK FOR YOURSELF: *How can people work to increase their patience in their lives?*

PUT IT INTO PRACTICE: *How can you make a positive and meaningful difference to the world, however small or large it may be?*

Lesson 94

What May Seem Like a Crushing Blow Now May Seem Like a Little Tap Later

In the course of a normal career, you will encounter many successes, but also many failures. At the time, some of these failures may seem spectacular. I mentioned earlier the time I thought I had a job offer from another university, told Yale I did, and then found I didn't. All I wanted to do was bury my head in the sand. At another point in my career, I seemed to be building up a stream of rejections of articles that would set a world record. When such things happen, they may seem like the end of the world. You may feel like quitting. Don't! What seems like a world-shattering failure at one point, in retrospect years, months, or sometimes, even weeks later will not seem so important. You just have to get through these difficult times with all the dignity you can preserve.

Often you will feel like other people are thinking about and talking about nothing other than your failures. Chances are that you are exaggerating other people's interest in you. But the passage of time cures many wounds. Just let time take its course, and above all, preserve your dignity in doing so.

Many of the most successful writers, artists, and scientists have had stunningly bad periods in their lives. They have endured deaths in the family, major public scandals, critical rejection of their work, and on the list goes. But the ones who "made it" did not give up. I noticed at one point that many novels by one of my favorite writers, Dean Koontz, were reissues of novels that had been published earlier under a different title. At first, I was puzzled. Then I figured out what had happened. The novels were published before Koontz became a best-selling writer. In those days, they did not sell much. Now, reissued with new titles, their sales were excellent. Imagine the loss to the world if Koontz had given up in the face of low sales.

I have had a few crushing blows in my life. My father walked out of our house when I was 16, never to return or make any effort to see me. I've had crucial grant proposals turned down. I've had a job blow up in my face. I'm still here. Truly, one of the major factors in career and life success is resilience—just getting through the hard times to the better times ahead.

THINK FOR YOURSELF: *Why do blows in life often seem worse at first than they do later on?*

PUT IT INTO PRACTICE: *Have you had any major blows in your life? How have you dealt with them? Have you found a way to get through them? Five years later, did they seem as serious as they did at the time? Do you have the grit and the guts to keep going in the face of what, at a given time, may seem like almost insurmountable obstacles?*

Lesson 95
Be Programmatic in Your Work

When psychology departments make decisions about hiring, one of the things they look for in a candidate is not just a body of research but also a program of research. A *research program* is an organized plan that seeks to develop a set of ideas to answer a set of questions that evolve one from another. For example, in my own career I started off studying the information-processing components of intelligence as it is traditionally defined (Sternberg, 1977, 1983). Then I began to believe that the traditional definition of intelligence was too narrow, because there are intelligent people who have little common sense, or what I called practical intelligence. Then I realized that some people were traditionally (i.e., analytically) and practically intelligent, too, but rarely or never seemed to have any meaningful ideas of their own. So I came to study creative intelligence, and onward the research program went.

It is not necessary that all the research you do be programmatic. Many researchers, in the course of a career, come upon ideas do not fit into any program of research, and they pursue these ideas simply because they are interested in finding the answers. But, generally, the research with the highest payoff is that which falls into a programmatic line.

Sometimes research that initially seems like it will be merely a sideline becomes a major program of research. In my own case, I collaborated with a student in a study of love (Sternberg & Grajek, 1984), expecting when

I started this work to do just the one set of studies and not return to the topic. But I found that one idea led to another, and soon I was involved in a program of research that culminated in several books (e.g., Sternberg, 1998b, 1998c; Sternberg & Weis, 2006).

At other times, research that you hope will lead to a full-fledged research program fizzles out. In the 1980s, I had some ideas about conflict resolution, and the ideas resulted in two publications in a well-known and well-regarded journal (Sternberg & Dobson, 1987; Sternberg & Soriano, 1984). I then had some other ideas, but I did not feel that anything was particularly exciting about them. It seemed as though I had rather quickly reached a dead end. So I brought this incipient program of research to a close, at least temporarily. One rarely knows, in beginning a research program, whether it will prove to be highly productive or simply transitory. In this case, the research program proved to be transitory. Transitory research programs are fine, but ultimately, people who are remembered typically are those who have, at some point, established systematic programs of research.

THINK FOR YOURSELF: *Are there any disadvantages to programmatic research in science?*

PUT IT INTO PRACTICE: *Are you programmatic in your research? That is, does the research tell a story? If not, what is the story you most would like to tell? How could you translate it into a program of research?*

Lesson 96
All Bad Times Come to an End

For better or for worse, you will always, in a career, end up having to do things you neither like to do nor do particularly well. In some periods, the bad things seem never to end. I am no great fan of long meetings, but I sit through countless long meetings. Sometimes I go through periods where it seems to be all meetings, all the time. You are best-off recognizing the things that you don't like, and being reasonably cheerful about them. If you find this difficult, look at these undesired things as a tax you pay for being in a career you (hopefully) really enjoy. All jobs have such taxes: There is no perfect job. But just as you have to pay your taxes in full to the government, you have to pay your taxes in full to your job. Better times will come.

Sometimes you go through periods that are catastrophically bad. Everything seems to go wrong, perhaps in a short period. I've gone through several such periods. No matter what I did, it seemed to turn to crud. And what I didn't do—that turned to crud too. At times I've wondered whether such bad periods would ever come to an end. They do. But hanging in, waiting for such periods to let up, can be very painful. Sometimes there simply is no substitute for patience and hope.

When I was in graduate school, I used to wonder what it was that distinguished those who reached high levels of success in their careers from those who did not. As the years went by, I came to see it was not their IQs, or whether they had fancy degrees, or whether they had had a good idea at one point or another. Rather, what everyone has in common is that, sooner or later, one encounters challenging life circumstances—the death of a parent, divorce, illness, failure to get tenure, serious injury, or whatever. In my experience, the people who succeed—who are high in what I called *successful intelligence* (Sternberg, 2003)—are those who can recover from these catastrophic events. They are able to bounce back and move on. That's the challenge we all face in our lives, usually multiple times.

THINK FOR YOURSELF: *Why, when things are going wrong, do we feel like this never will end?*

PUT IT INTO PRACTICE: *How do you recover from awful events in your life? Are there things you could do to recover more quickly or more fully?*

Lesson 97
Know When To Move On in Your Work and When Not to

I once attended a presentation by a colleague who was about 10 years post-PhD. She was describing her attempts to prove a certain thesis. The problem was that she had been trying for the entire 10 years of her career to prove this thesis, and her research program was going nowhere. Yet she would not give up. I don't think her career has gone very far since. Perhaps she is still trying to prove the same thesis.

There is a fine line between perseverance and perseveration. *Perseverance* occurs when you keep trying to reach your goals in the face of obstacles. *Perseveration* occurs when you keep trying to reach your goals, in the absence of any evidence, over a period of time, that these goals are getting any closer to being reached. You need to know when to give up.

Sometimes you give up for a given time. For years, I was interested in studying wisdom but could not find an angle. I had some tentative ideas about ways of approaching the problem, but they did not seem to lead very far. I began to see that my attempts were getting me nowhere, so after one or two such attempts, I decided to put the study of wisdom aside and move on to other things. Some years later, I saw what I thought was an avenue of research for studying wisdom and I again started actively studying it. But I was glad I had left time to incubate on the problem, because I just was not ready to study it earlier on.

□ □ □ □ □ □ □

THINK FOR YOURSELF: *Why are people often
afraid to move on in their lives?*

PUT IT INTO PRACTICE: *Do you know, in your life and
in your work in particular, when it is time to move on?
What are the clues you use to suggest that you need to
turn a new page in your work or your life in general?*

Lesson 98
Strive for Impact

Every once in a while, I am asked what I am trying to achieve in my career. Chances are, you will be asked too, at some point. Although you obviously do not have to answer the question, it might be worthwhile to consider if you do have any higher order goals, and if so, what they are.

I do have a higher order professional goal, which is to strive for impact—on science, on education, and on society. Indeed, for me, the meaning that life has is that the world be a somewhat different place for my having been in it. I do not claim this is the meaning everyone should assign. My personal goal is to see my wife and five children find happiness and success in their lives, according to whatever they mean by *success*. Perhaps other meanings are just as good.

My own satisfaction is directly related to the impact I can have. For some people, societal goals are less important than scientific advancement for its own sake. When I look at the power science has to be used for either good or for evil, I believe that all of us should consider how to use science to improve society rather than hurt it. The development of wisdom in people seems not to have kept up with the development of technology, and society desperately needs for wisdom to catch up, before society destroys itself. Before September 11, 2001, such words might have seemed Cassandra-like and perhaps unnecessarily pessimistic. Today they perhaps seem more realistic. The world is what we make it, and we can make it better or worse as we choose.

There are many different ways to have impact. I hope that my work in intelligence, creativity, wisdom, and love has impact. But I have decided that the most important impact I ever will have will be through raising five children, as I mentioned previously. They will live on long after I'm gone. We each have to strive for impact in our own way: There is no one size that fits all.

THINK FOR YOURSELF: *How should people decide what is meaningful to them to accomplish in their lives?*

PUT IT INTO PRACTICE: *How have you had an impact on the lives of others? How might you have even more of an impact in the future?*

Lesson 99
Seek To Be Remembered for Your Positive, Not Negative, Contributions

During my first year as an assistant professor, I became interested in a problem that my faculty mentor, Wendell Garner, was studying, namely, whether structure is in the stimulus or in the interaction between people's perception of the stimulus and the actual stimulus. I believed then, and believe now, that structure is in the interaction. Garner, however, was to some extent a follower of Jimmy Gibson, the great psychologist of perception, and believed that large amounts of structure reside in the stimulus.

I did a study that I thought was a nice demonstration that Garner was wrong. The study did not directly support the interactionist position but did seem to me to undermine the stimulus-based position. I wrote up the article, criticizing Garner's position on the basis of my data. That was a pretty gutsy thing for me to do, given that Garner was a senior faculty member and also chair of the department!

I submitted the article to a journal, and it got rejected. Not letting myself be fazed, I presented the contents of the article as a talk to the group of Saul Sternberg (no relation to me) at Bell Labs in Murray Hill, New Jersey. After the talk, Sternberg raised a point regarding my data that I had missed. This was the one time in my life—at least so far—that a comment just utterly demolished a talk. I realized that he was right, and that my data actually showed nothing at all. I was totally humiliated and only wished that I would instantly disappear.

No trap door opened, and Sternberg was very kind and genial about the whole thing. I went back and felt a need to apologize to Garner, because of course he knew about the work I was doing. A lesser scholar and a lesser person would have held what I did against me. He didn't. Instead, he told me, in his avuncular style, that I had an important lesson to learn, namely, that scientists are judged primarily by the positive contributions they make, not by the negative ones. This was great advice.

Some people try to build a career attacking others. In essence, they try to ride on the coattails of others, hoping to attract attention to themselves by attacking people, usually ones who are considerably better known than they are. I have had the honor of being attacked by several such people over the course of my career. I say "honor" because these people do not bother to attack you unless they think you are well-enough known to bring them attention.

After Garner gave me his advice, my whole attitude toward the field of psychology changed. I realized that the attack dog mentality really does not bring one very far. Moreover, as Kuhn (2012) pointed out, new paradigms tend to replace old paradigms not when the old paradigms are merely criticized but when better or at least more currently useful ideas take their place.

This is not to say that you should never criticize anyone's research. Part of almost any research career will involve disagreeing with other people. The important thing is to have a better idea yourself—something that replaces or builds on what they have done.

▣ ▣ ▣ ▣ ▣ ▣ ▣

THINK FOR YOURSELF: *What are the advantages of seeking to make positive contributions to the world rather than making contributions through disparaging others?*

PUT IT INTO PRACTICE: *Do you tend to be someone who finds the good in things or the bad in them? How can you ensure that the contribution you make in the world is a positive rather than a negative one?*

Lesson 100
Go Your Own Way and the Rewards Will Follow

Some years back, I edited a book titled *Psychologists Defying the Crowd: Stories of Those Who Battled the Establishments and Won* (Sternberg, 2002b). The main point of the book is that creative scientists defy the scientific establishment (Sternberg, 1999; Sternberg & Lubart, 1995; see also Sternberg, Fiske, & Foss, in press). Such scientists may choose to go their own way with respect to theory, research paradigm, philosophical orientation, or subject matter studied. The risks can be great because the cost of such defiance can be rejected articles, unfunded grant proposals, and, in extreme cases, scientific oblivion. Yet, these scientists—individuals such as Wundt, Freud, and Binet—are often and perhaps usually the ones whose work lives on, whereas the work of those scientists who pandered to existing scientific tastes often (although certainly not always) dies with them.

For young scientists in general and for psychologists in particular, the pressure to conform is great. Rejection rates of journals and granting agencies in psychology are among the highest of any field, and reviews by referees are sometimes the most vicious. Radically nonconforming work is less likely to be accepted. Young scientists typically have only 5 to 7 years before they reach an up-or-out decision for tenure, and even graduate students may find that working within the research paradigms of their mentors is substantially safer than finding their own way when they seek a letter of recommendation. There are other ways to make contributions besides journal articles—teaching, service, writing books, giving talks—but in psychological science, as of 2016, writing articles is still one of the prime ways.

Scientists who defy the crowd are rare because there is so much pressure to conform. In the short term, the rewards of conformity are great: easier job placement or promotion, better funding, easier acceptance of journal submissions book proposals, approbation of colleagues, and a sense of affiliation with the crowd. In the long run, however, the rewards of creative nonconformity may be substantially greater.

My book lists many good examples of psychologists who defied the crowd and won (Sternberg, 2002b; for examples from other fields, see Sternberg, Kaufman, & Pretz, 2002, and Sternberg & Lubart, 1995). Ellen Berscheid was pilloried by a senator, by many in the press, and even by some of her colleagues for having the audacity to study love in a scientific way. She received death threats. Today she has won most of the major awards in psychology, including the American Psychological Association (APA) Distinguished Scientific Contribution Award, for her landmark contributions to the psychology of interpersonal attraction. Indeed, together with Elaine Hatfield, she practically originated the field of the social psychology of love, as we now know it. For quite a while, John Garcia was unable to publish some of his work on conditioning in any major journal. His findings that learning could occur within one trial and that the nature of the reinforcement does matter were so controversial that many psychologists refused to accept them. Reviewers were reluctant to accept work in journals that seemed to be so dubious with respect to its likely validity. He, too, later became a winner of the APA Distinguished Scientific Contribution Award. The point is that resisting the temptation to follow the crowd can be a winning strategy if one has the right ideas and, perhaps just as important, the guts to stick with them.

I have had an experience in my career that was an eye-opener with regard to going my own way and defying the crowd. I was funded by a large testing organization to do research on college admissions (see Sternberg, 2010a). The idea was to see whether a supplement to traditional college-admissions tests could improve prediction of academic performance. The results were great: My colleagues and I more than doubled prediction over a commonly used standardized test. I figured now I would get the "big money." I figured wrong. When the organization saw that the project was highly successful and greatly improved prediction over its own test, the organization shut the project down. I'll let you figure out why.

The biggest problem, of course, is knowing when to defy the crowd and when not to. There is no ironclad set of rules for knowing. However, here are some tips that may be useful. The more questions you answer *yes* to, the more likely it is you should defy the crowd.

- Is the issue a matter of principle?
- Is the issue one you care deeply about?
- Is the issue an important one—for you, for others, for science, for society?
- Have you considered all possible issues in coming to your position?
- Do you have credible arguments to support your position?
- Will there be significant adverse consequences if you fail to defy the crowd?
- Are you confident of the rightness of your position?
- Will your conscience bother you if you fail to defy the crowd?
- Is there any reasonable chance of recruiting others to take your position?
- Are you willing to fight for your position, come what may?

◨ ◨ ◨ ◨ ◨ ◨ ◨

THINK FOR YOURSELF: *Why do journal articles play such an important role in psychological science, now, as much as many years ago?*

PUT IT INTO PRACTICE: *What is your way? If you do not know, how will you find out?*

Lesson 101
Knowledge Is
a Double-Edged Sword

Some years ago, I was visiting a very famous psychologist who lives abroad. As part of the tour he had planned for me, he invited me to visit the local zoo. We went past the cages of the primates, who were, at the time, engaged in what euphemistically could be called unexpected sexual behavior. I, of course, averted my eyes. However, my host did not do the same. After observing the primates for a short time, he began to speak. I was astounded to hear him analyze the sexual behavior of the primates in terms of his theory of intelligence. It was as though he had come to see almost everything in terms of his theory of intelligence, applying the theory way beyond where it properly applied. In effect, his expertise had caused him to experience a kind of tunnel vision—a narrowing of his scope. I realized at that time, as I have many times since, how knowledge and expertise can be a double-edged sword.

On the one hand, one cannot be creative without knowledge. Quite simply, one cannot go beyond the existing state of knowledge if one does not know what that state is. Many students have ideas that are creative with respect to themselves but not with respect to the field because others have had the same ideas before. Those with a greater knowledge base can be creative in ways that those who are still learning about the basics of the field cannot be.

At the same time, those who have an expert level of knowledge can experience tunnel vision, narrow thinking, and entrenchment. Experts can

Psychology 101½: The Unspoken Rules for Success in Academia, Second Edition, by R. J. Sternberg
Copyright © 2017 by the American Psychological Association. All rights reserved.

become so stuck in a way of thinking that they become unable to extricate themselves from it. Such narrowing does not just happen to others. It happens to everyone, myself included. For example, at one point in my career, every theory I proposed seemed to have three parts. (Of course, there were three good reasons for this . . .) At that point, I was stuck on threes. Learning must be a lifelong process, not one that terminates when a person achieves some measure of recognition. When a person believes that he or she knows everything there is to know, he or she is unlikely to ever show truly meaningful creativity again.

The upshot is that I tell my students that the teaching–learning process is a two-way process. I have as much to learn from my students as they have to learn from me. I have knowledge they do not have, but they have flexibility I do not have—precisely because they do not know as much as I do. By learning from, as well as teaching to, one's students, one opens up channels for creativity that otherwise would remain closed.

If a student has an idea that I don't like, I will tell him or her. But I will also acknowledge that it's only my opinion, and I may be wrong. I will encourage the student to present at one of our two weekly meetings, and as often as not, others will see value I do not see. We all can become imprisoned by our own expertise. But we also can free ourselves of this prison if only we choose to do so.

THINK FOR YOURSELF: *How can knowledge interfere with creativity?*

PUT IT INTO PRACTICE: *Have you ever found your knowledge a hindrance to your moving forward? What steps do you take to keep yourself from getting stuck in your work or career? Are there other steps you could take?*

Lesson 101½
Don't Just Read It, Do It

I hope you have benefited from the lessons in this book. So here is my last piece of advice: Don't just read it, do it! Your life is yours to live as you wish. I hope that the knowledge I have gained through the years will help you make the very best possible of your career and your life. Good luck! Whatever it is you want in life, go for it!

Psychology 101½: The Unspoken Rules for Success in Academia, Second Edition, by R. J. Sternberg

References

Argyris, C. (2012). *Organizational traps*. New York, NY: Oxford University Press.

Cianciolo, A. T., Matthew, C. T., Sternberg, R. J., & Wagner, R. A. (2006). Tacit knowledge, practical intelligence, and expertise. In N. Charness, K. A. Ericsson, P. Feltovich, & R. Hoffman (Eds.), *Cambridge handbook of expertise and expert performance* (pp. 613–632). http://dx.doi.org/10.1017/CBO9780511816796.035

Cohen, J., & Cohen, P. (2002). *Applied multiple regression/correlation analysis for the behavioral sciences* (3rd ed.). Hillsdale, NJ: Erlbaum.

Cronbach, L. J. (1957). The two disciplines of scientific psychology. *American Psychologist, 12*, 671–684. http://dx.doi.org/10.1037/h0043943

Ericsson, K. A. (1996). The acquisition of expert performance: An introduction to some of the issues. In K. A. Ericsson (Ed.), *The road to excellence: The acquisition of expert performance in the arts and sciences, sports, and games* (pp. 1–50). Mahwah, NJ: Erlbaum.

Ericsson, K. A. (Ed.). (2009). *Development of professional expertise*. http://dx.doi.org/10.1017/CBO9780511609817

Flynn, J. R. (2012). *Are we getting smarter? Rising IQ in the twenty-first century*. New York, NY: Cambridge University Press.

Gardner, H. (1999). *Intelligence reframed: Multiple intelligences for the 21st century*. New York, NY: Basic Books.

Gardner, H. (2011). *Frames of mind: The theory of multiple intelligences* (3rd ed.). New York, NY: Basic Books.

Garner, W. R., Hake, H. W., & Eriksen, C. W. (1956). Operationism and the concept of perception. *Psychological Review, 63*, 149–159. http://dx.doi.org/10.1037/h0042992

Gilovich, T., Vallone, R., & Tversky, A. (1985). The hot hand in basketball: On the misperception of random sequences. *Cognitive Psychology, 17*, 295–314. http://dx.doi.org/10.1016/0010-0285(85)90010-6

Kahneman, D. (2013). *Thinking, fast and slow*. New York, NY: Farrar, Straus, & Giroux.

Kuhn, T. S. (2012). *The structure of scientific revolutions* (4th ed.). http://dx.doi.org/ 10.7208/chicago/9780226458144.001.0001

Langer, E. J. (2014). *The power of mindful learning.* New York, NY: Da Capo.

Latané, B., & Darley, J. (1970). *The unresponsive bystander: Why doesn't he help?* New York, NY: Appleton-Century-Crofts.

Milgram, S. (2009). *Obedience to authority: An experimental view.* New York, NY: Harper Perennial.

Mischel, W. (2014). *The marshmallow test: Mastering self-control.* New York, NY: Little-Brown.

Pinker, S. (2014). *The sense of style.* New York, NY: Viking.

Ronson, J. (2015). *So you've been publicly shamed.* New York, NY: Riverhead.

Seligman, M. (2006). *Learned optimism.* New York, NY: Vintage.

Seligman, M. (in press). How positive psychology happened and where it is going. In R. J. Sternberg, S. T. Fiske, & D. J. Foss (Eds.), *Psychologists making a difference: One hundred eminent behavioral and brain scientists talk about their most important contributions.* New York, NY: Cambridge University Press.

Siegler, R. S. (1992). The other Alfred Binet. *Developmental Psychology, 28,* 179–190. http://dx.doi.org/10.1037/0012-1649.28.2.179

Simonton, D. K. (1997). Creative productivity: A predictive and explanatory model for caret trajectories and landmarks. *Psychological Review, 104,* 66–89. http:// dx.doi.org/10.1037/0033-295X.104.1.66

Simonton, D. K. (2004). *Creativity in science.* http://dx.doi.org/10.1017/ CBO9781139165358

Sonnenfeld, J., & Ward, A. (2007). *Fighting back: How great leaders rebound after career disasters.* Boston, MA: Harvard Business Review Press.

Sternberg, R. J. (1977). *Intelligence, information processing, and analogical reasoning: The componential analysis of human abilities.* Hillsdale, NJ: Erlbaum.

Sternberg, R. J. (1983). Components of human intelligence. *Cognition, 15,* 1–48. http://dx.doi.org/10.1016/0010-0277(83)90032-X

Sternberg, R. J. (1985). *Beyond IQ: A triarchic theory of human intelligence.* New York, NY: Cambridge University Press.

Sternberg, R. J. (1986). *Intelligence applied: Understanding and increasing your intellectual skills.* San Diego, CA: Harcourt Brace Jovanovich.

Sternberg, R. J. (1997a). *Successful intelligence.* New York, NY: Plume.

Sternberg, R. J. (1997b). *Thinking styles.* http://dx.doi.org/10.1017/ CBO9780511584152

Sternberg, R. J. (1998a). A balance theory of wisdom. *Review of General Psychology, 2,* 347–365. http://dx.doi.org/10.1037/1089-2680.2.4.347

Sternberg, R. J. (1998b). *Cupid's arrow: The course of love through time.* New York, NY: Cambridge University Press.

Sternberg, R. J. (1998c). *Love is a story.* New York, NY: Oxford University Press.

Sternberg, R. J. (1999). A propulsion model of types of creative contributions. *Review of General Psychology, 3,* 83–100. http://dx.doi.org/10.1037/ 1089-2680.3.2.83

Sternberg, R. J. (2000). *Making school reform work: A "mineralogical" theory of school modifiability.* Bloomington, IN: Phi Delta Kappa Educational Foundation.

Sternberg, R. J. (2001). Why schools should teach for wisdom: The balance theory of wisdom in educational settings. *Educational Psychologist, 36,* 227–245. http://dx.doi.org/10.1207/S15326985EP3604_2

Sternberg, R. J. (2002a). Everything you need to know to understand the current controversies you learned from psychological research: A comment on the Rind and Lilienfeld controversies. *American Psychologist, 57,* 193–197. http://dx.doi.org/10.1037/0003-066X.57.3.193

Sternberg, R. J. (Ed.). (2002b). *Psychologists defying the crowd: Stories of those who battled the establishment and won.* Washington, DC: American Psychological Association.

Sternberg, R. J. (Ed.). (2002c). *Why smart people can be so stupid.* New Haven, CT: Yale University Press.

Sternberg, R. J. (2003). *Wisdom, intelligence, and creativity.* http://dx.doi.org/ 10.1017/CBO9780511509612

Sternberg, R. J. (2006). Is there still any hope of a unified psychology? *The General Psychologist, 41,* 15–16.

Sternberg, R. J. (2008). It's the foolishness, stupid. *The American Interest, 4,* 19–23. Retrieved from http://www.the-american-interest.com/2008/09/01/ its-the-foolishness-stupid/

Sternberg, R. J. (2010a). *College admissions for the 21st century.* Cambridge, MA: Harvard University Press.

Sternberg, R. J. (2010b). Teaching for creativity. In R. A. Beghetto & J. C. Kaufman (Eds.), *Nurturing creativity in the classroom* (pp. 394–414). http://dx.doi.org/ 10.1017/CBO9780511781629.020

Sternberg, R. J. (2011). The theory of successful intelligence. In R. J. Sternberg & S. B. Kaufman (Eds.), *Cambridge handbook of intelligence* (pp. 504–527). http://dx.doi.org/10.1017/CBO9780511977244.026

Sternberg, R. J. (2012). Intelligence in its cultural context. In M. Gelfand, C.-Y. Chiu, & Y.-Y. Hong (Eds.), *Advances in cultures and psychology* (Vol. 2, pp. 205–248). http://dx.doi.org/10.1093/acprof:oso/9780199840694.003.0005

Sternberg, R. J. (2013). Personal wisdom in the balance. In M. Ferrari & N. Weststrate (Eds.), *The scientific study of personal wisdom: From contemplative traditions to neuroscience* (pp. 53–74). New York, NY: Springer.

Sternberg, R. J. (2015). Epilogue: Why is ethical behavior challenging? A model of ethical reasoning. In R. J. Sternberg & S. T. Fiske (Eds.), *Ethical challenges in the behavioral and brain sciences* (pp. 219–226). http://dx.doi.org/ 10.1017/CBO9781139626491.082

Sternberg, R. J., & Dobson, D. M. (1987). Resolving interpersonal conflicts: An analysis of stylistic consistency. *Journal of Personality and Social Psychology, 52,* 794–812. http://dx.doi.org/10.1037/0022-3514.52.4.794

Sternberg, R. J., & Fiske, S. E. (Eds.). (2015). *Ethical challenges in the behavioral and brain sciences: Case studies and commentaries.* http://dx.doi.org/10.1017/CBO9781139626491

Sternberg, R. J., Fiske, S. T., & Foss, D. J. (Eds.). (in press). *Psychologists making a difference: One hundred eminent behavioral and brain scientists talk about their most important contributions.* New York, NY: Cambridge University Press.

Sternberg, R. J., Forsythe, G. B., Hedlund, J., Horvath, J., Snook, S., Williams, W. M., . . . Grigorenko, E. L. (2000). *Practical intelligence in everyday life.* New York, NY: Cambridge University Press.

Sternberg, R. J., & Grajek, S. (1984). The nature of love. *Journal of Personality and Social Psychology, 47,* 312–329.

Sternberg, R. J., & Grigorenko, E. L. (2007). *Teaching for successful intelligence: To increase student learning and achievement* (2nd ed.). Thousand Oaks, CA: Corwin Press.

Sternberg, R. J., Grigorenko, E. L., & Zhang, L.-F. (2008). Styles of learning and thinking matter in instruction and assessment. *Perspectives on Psychological Science, 3,* 486–506. http://dx.doi.org/10.1111/j.1745-6924.2008.00095.x

Sternberg, R. J., Jarvin, L., & Grigorenko, E. L. (2009). *Teaching for wisdom, intelligence, creativity, and success.* http://dx.doi.org/10.4135/9781483350608

Sternberg, R. J., Kaufman, J. C., & Grigorenko, E. L. (2008). *Intelligence applied* (2nd ed.). http://dx.doi.org/10.1017/CBO9780511611445

Sternberg, R. J., Kaufman, J. C., & Pretz, J. E. (2002). *The creativity conundrum: A propulsion model of kinds of creative contributions.* New York, NY: Psychology Press.

Sternberg, R. J., & Lubart, T. I. (1995). *Defying the crowd: Cultivating creativity in a culture of conformity.* New York, NY: Free Press.

Sternberg, R. J., Nokes, K., Geissler, P. W., Prince, R., Okatcha, F., Bundy, D. A., & Grigorenko, E. L. (2001). The relationship between academic and practical intelligence: A case study in Kenya. *Intelligence, 29,* 401–418. http://dx.doi.org/10.1016/S0160-2896(01)00065-4

Sternberg, R. J., & Soriano, L. J. (1984). Styles of conflict resolution. *Journal of Personality and Social Psychology, 47,* 115–126. http://dx.doi.org/10.1037/0022-3514.47.1.115

Sternberg, R. J., & Sternberg, K. (in press). *The psychologist's companion* (6th ed.). New York, NY: Cambridge University Press.

Sternberg, R. J., & Weis, K. (Eds.). (2006). *The new psychology of love.* New Haven, CT: Yale University Press.

Tan, M. T., Aljughaiman, A. M., Elliott, J. G., Kornilov, S. A., Ferrando Prieto, M., Bolden, D. S., . . . Grigorenko, E. L. (2009). Considering language, culture, and cognitive abilities. In E. L. Grigorenko (Ed.), *Multicultural psychoeducational assessment* (pp. 443–468). New York, NY: Springer.

Tulving, E. (1966). Subjective organization and effects of repetition in multitrial free-recall learning. *Journal of Verbal Learning and Verbal Behavior, 19,* 242–252.

Tulving, E., & Thomson, D. M. (1973). Encoding specificity and retrieval processes in episodic memory. *Psychological Review, 80,* 352–373. http://dx.doi.org/10.1037/h0020071

Tversky, A., & Kahneman, D. (1973). Availability: A heuristic for judging frequency and probability. *Cognitive Psychology, 5,* 207–232. http://dx.doi.org/10.1016/0010-0285(73)90033-9

Zuckerman, H. (1983). The scientific elite: Nobel laureates' mutual influences. In R. S. Albert (Ed.), *Genius and eminence: The social psychology of creativity and exceptional achievement* (Vol. 5, pp. 241–252). New York, NY: Pergamon.

Index

About the Author

Robert J. Sternberg, PhD, received his BA from Yale and his doctorate from Stanford. He also is the recipient of 13 honorary doctorates. He is a professor of human development at Cornell University. Prior to that, he served as a university dean, provost, and president. Earlier, Dr. Sternberg was IBM Professor of Psychology and Education in the Department of Psychology at Yale University and director of the Yale Center for the Psychology of Abilities, Competencies, and Expertise (PACE Center). He was also the 2003 president of the American Psychological Association and the 2012–2013 president of the Federation of Associations in Behavioral and Brain Sciences. He is editor of *Perspectives on Psychological Science* and previously was editor of *Contemporary Psychology: APA Review of Books* and *Psychological Bulletin*. He has won many awards, including the James McKeen Cattell Award of the Association for Psychological Science. Dr. Sternberg is a member of the American Academy of Arts and Sciences and the National Academy of Education.